Barry Krisberg teaches in the School of Criminology at the University of California, Berkeley. He has written a monograph *The Gang and the Community* and a number of articles in journals such as *Social Policy, Issues in Criminology,* and *Crime and Social Justice.* Krisberg is vice-president of the Western Division of the American Society of Criminology. He is an editor of *Crime and Social Justice.*

Crime and Privilege

Toward a New Criminology

BARRY KRISBERG

Prentice-Hall, Inc. Englewood Cliffs, New Jersey

Library of Congress Cataloging in Publication Data

Krisberg, Barry.
Crime and privilege.

(A Spectrum book)
Bibliography: p.
Includes index.
1. Crime and criminals. I. Title.
HV6030.K75 364 75-12839
ISBN 0-13-192740-X
ISBN 0-13-192732-9 pbk.

A Spectrum Book

10 9 8 7 6 5 4 3 2 1

Printed in the United States of America

Prentice-Hall International, Inc., *London*
Prentice-Hall of Australia Pty. Ltd., *Sydney*
Prentice-Hall of Canada Ltd., *Toronto*
Prentice-Hall of India Private Limited, *New Delhi*
Prentice-Hall of Japan, Inc., *Tokyo*
Prentice-Hall of Southeast Asia (Pte.) Ltd., *Singapore*

For my parents, for Rose Samuel,
and especially for Karen.

Contents

Acknowledgements

The author is especially indebted to Karen Leslie McKie, who contributed a great deal of time to the development and improvement of this book. Several colleagues at the School of Criminology, University of California, Berkeley, helped the author with their comments and suggestions. Particular thanks go to Paul Takagi, Tony Platt, and Elliott Currie. I also wish to thank Barbara Arnold, who read an early draft of the manuscript. Karen Baily, Linda Peachee, and Florence Amamoto helped by typing most of the manuscript.

Michael Hunter, Barbara Smith, and William Setten of Prentice-Hall helped tremendously, and their patience with a youthful author is appreciated.

Finally, I must thank The Grant Street Irregulars, led by Beau Watson and Adam Sobig, for spiritual support through a long spring and summer of writing.

ONE

The Promise of the New Criminology

> We are often the unconscious prisoners of our type of society, of the conflicts occurring in it and of their hegemonic nature; we are not able to articulate and state thoughts which would liberate us and would help our institutions out of their vicious circle.
>
> **Marie Bertrand**

An important development in modern criminology is the ever-increasing number of researchers who find little or no value in the intellectual perspectives they inherited from their elders and teachers. Although their doubts may confuse and frustrate more seasoned criminologists, this open questioning of basic assumptions and philosophies that have dominated liberal criminology promises to expose hidden bias and to make implicit bias more explicit, and will perhaps result in a science of crime and crime control that is both moral and intellectually honest.

Life is not as simple as the stereotypes given us by the mass media; it is not simply a morality play of cops and robbers. It is a complexity that intrudes itself upon us when we reflect on the obvious inequities of our system of criminal justice, on our own experiences as law violators or victims, and on the criminality of some of our highest political leaders.

An expanded version of this chapter appeared as "The Sociological Imagination Revisited" (Krisberg, 1974). The author wishes to thank Isami and Dexter Waugh, Paul Takagi, Tony Platt, Marie Bertrand, and Karen McKie for their thoughtful suggestions.

Examples of this complexity pervade our society. The woman who is raped undergoes a series of degradations if she decides to report the offense to the authorities. She is treated as a contributor to the victimization and must *prove her innocence* to police and court officials who are paid to protect her. National surveys reveal that most persons do not report crimes to the police because they believe it will do no good. The poor, people of color, the young, and other oppressed groups view the police as agents of repression who abuse and constrain their attempts at self-determination. Daily, newspaper headlines tell of corruption and abuse of power by social control agents as well as the highest public officials. Social activists are jailed. Moreover, attempts to rehabilitate and help offenders seem to engender violence and antagonism. Some observers assert that our laws serve only a small ruling class. Public officials tell us of the contradiction of protecting individual rights versus the rights of society. Crime control efforts involve the building of great stores of weaponry, the massive invasion of privacy, and the specter of a garrison state.

Criminology, the systematic study of crime and crime control, should help us understand these contradictions about individual and social justice. Research in this area should help us clarify the underlying issues and alternatives so that we can make informed and humanistic judgments about crime and social control. The promise of the New Criminology is to link the study of crime with the larger pursuit of social justice and thus to aid in struggles to achieve human liberation from various forms of social oppression. The search for new perspectives in criminology has been activated and enriched by the ideas and practice of those committed to changing long-standing social injustices.

> the roots [of the New Criminology] are to be found in political struggles—the civil rights movement, the anti-war movement, the student movement, Third World liberation struggles inside as well as outside the United States, and anti-imperialist movements—and in the writings of the participants in these struggles—George Jackson (1970, 1972), Angela Davis (1971), Eldridge Cleaver (1968), Tom Hayden (1970), Sam Melville (1971), Bobby Seale (1968), Huey Newton (1973), Malcolm X (1964), and Ruchell Magee, to name a few. (Platt, 1974:1)

The task of building a New Criminology is hardly easy. One reason for this is the virtual stranglehold exercised by the guardians of the older heritage over funding sources and publication. In spite of the lack of funding and the difficulty in having their work published, some criminologists have performed the extremely crucial task of uncovering and exposing much of the racist, ideological, and oppressive work of many traditional criminologists. Snodgrass (1972) and Boostrom (1974), in as yet unpublished dissertations, have unpacked much of the ideology of the giants of American criminology. Taylor, Walton, and Young (1973) set out to debunk a wide range of classical and contemporary theories of criminology. Earlier works by Quinney (1970) and Matza (1969) have helped unravel the hidden ideologies of some criminologists. These authors have performed a useful function in clearing the path to what C. Wright Mills called "the sociological imagination"; these scholars have looked carefully and proclaimed loudly that the emperor has no clothes.

C. Wright Mills, the Sociological Imagination, and the New Criminology

Mills was an important thinker in the creation of the New Left and in the extension of radical analysis to sociology. Although Mills was not a criminologist per se, his writings in that field continue to be valued by the scholars of the New Criminology. His essay, "The Professional Ideology of the Social Pathologists" (1943), is a classic illustration of the ideological, biased character of texts on social problems. In this essay Mills demonstrated how the particular value system of small-town, rural Protestantism was used to define normality. Any person or group that did not conform to the ideals of small-town white, Protestant culture was labeled a social problem. For example, texts on social problems dealt with immigration as a problem of Americanizing newcomers to the United States. Rarely, if ever, did the social pathologists examine the racist sentiment of immigration legislation or the way in which immigration laws were used to harass and exploit foreign-born populations in this country. Mills argued that this ideology was rooted in the sameness of the social pathologists.

> If the members of an academic profession are recruited from similar social contexts and if their backgrounds and careers are similar, there is a tendency for them to be uniformly set for some common perspective. The common conditions of their profession often seem more important in this connection than similarity of extraction. Within such a homogeneous group there tend to be fewer divergent points of view which would clash

> over the meaning of facts and thus give rise to interpretations on a more theoretical level. (Mills, in Horowitz, 1967:527)

The ideology of most criminologists can be understood in terms of their class, sexual, and racial sameness. It is likewise clear that this sameness distorts studies of the criminal and gives life to the stereotype of the criminal as being clearly inferior from the social pathologist.

Mills also provided valuable insight into the phenomenon of upper-class vice (*Ibid.*, pp. 324–329). In this essay Mills showed how commercialized vice was used in the operation of big business. And in his master work, *The Power Elite* (1959a), Mills was one of the first American sociologists to describe the influence of the military-industrial establishment on our society. In that work Mills argued that political corruption should be understood in terms of a more general level of moral insensibility: "The higher immorality is a systematic feature of the American elite: its general acceptance is an essential feature of the mass society" (Mills, 1959a:343). Young men "on the make" in American politics must acquire a blunted sense of morality. Mills warned that "in economic and political institutions the corporate rich now wield enormous power, but they have never had to win the moral consent of those over whom they hold this power" (*Ibid.*, p. 344).

The development of a critical outlook is an important stage in the struggle for social justice, because myths are used to legitimate oppression.

> It is necessary for the oppressors to approach the people in order, via subjugation, to keep them passive. This approximation, however, does not involve being with the people, or require true communication. It is accomplished by the oppressors' depositing myths indispensable to the preservation of the status quo. (Freire, 1970:135)

Developing a critical perspective in criminology is particularly crucial because in the area of crime and crime control we encounter myths designed to legitimate the use of force to maintain order. Crime is defined, first and foremost, as an act against the political state. This is symbolized by the language used in legal prosecution—The State of New York versus John Smith. Crime myths include a definition of the state as morally blameless. The criminal is different, inferior, and dangerous. Criminal justice agencies are portrayed as above politics and fair in their interpretation of laws. The New Criminology directs us to ask basic questions about the quality of justice in our society; it asks us to evaluate the democracy of our political institutions, the fairness of our economic institutions, and the humanity of our social relationships. The nature of crime in our society and the quality of justice rendered by our legal institutions reveal fundamental facts about the overall fairness of our social structure. Investigating the relationship between crime and the maintenance of social privilege is thus central to the New Criminology. In posing questions and in seeking answers we are implicitly looking for alternative social arrangements. As one observer has noted, "If we are to remove the oppression of the age, we must critically understand the world around us" (Quinney, 1974:1). Conventional thinking about crime and crime control confirms the official ideology about the existing social order. To transcend traditional myths permits the consideration of alternatives to the present social order.

Mills's concept of the sociological imagination can be used to guide a New Criminology.

> Know that many personal troubles cannot be solved merely as troubles, but must be understood in terms of public issues and in terms of the problems of history making. Know that the human meaning of public issues must be revealed by relating them to personal troubles and to the problems of individual life. (Mills, 1959b:226)

Personal "troubles" are threats to values cherished by individuals. These occur within the "character of the individual and within the range of his immediate relations with others" (*Ibid.*, p. 8). Sociological studies of personal troubles suggests that we use biographical material in attempting to describe and understand the impact of these troubles upon humans. Autobiographies of a wide variety of persons who have been criminals or social control agents are available to the student. Prominent among autobiographies relevant to criminology are those of Malcolm X (1964), Piri Thomas (1967), Claude Brown (1965), and George Jackson (1972).[1]

American criminology has traditionally used the "delinquent's own story" as a research technique. Ultimately, however, criminologists have chosen to discredit the face value of autobiographic accounts as

[1] See also Duane Denfeld, ed., *Streetwise Criminology* (1974), an anthology of a wide range of writings by participants in the world of crime and criminal justice. This book also includes a rich bibliography of useful firsthand material. Peterson and Truzzi's *Criminal Life Views From Inside* (1972) is another excellent source with an extensive bibliography.

they pursue the correction of criminal offenders. Albert Morris pinpointed this attitude when he wrote in his survey of criminals' views of themselves, "Even when they are lacking in their penetration or sincerity, the verbalizations of criminals may have a diagnostic value as great as overt behavior" (Morris, 1941:139). Here we see a common element in most criminological writing, the tendency to denigrate or discredit the delinquent's view of social reality: officials are to listen to the criminal only as a means of diagnosing and changing him. In the process of denying the validity of criminals' firsthand accounts the traditional criminologist moved further away from understanding personal troubles, much less appreciating their relationship to public issues.

Issues, according to Mills, involve some values that are cherished by the public; such values overlap individual milieus. The study of issues requires investigation of how personal networks fit into the institutions of a society. Examples of issues are institutional racism, class injustices, the oppression of women, and the nature of the political economy.

Successful studies of the intersection of personal troubles and public issues include Fanon's essay, "Mental Disorders of Colonial Wars" (1969), Ben Tong's essay on Asian-Americans (1971), and Mills's *White Collar* (1956). A small but growing body of criminological literature exemplifies this key element of the sociological imagination. Let us examine two instances of the application of the sociological imagination to research on crime and delinquency, for this is the New Criminology.

Rape: The All-American Crime

The first example is Susan Griffin's essay, "Rape: The All-American Crime" (1971).[2] Ms. Griffin presents rape as a personal trouble in a most direct way by telling us of her fear and psychological confrontation with this crime.

> I have never been free of the fear of rape. From a very early age I, like most women, have thought of rape as part of my natural environment—something to be feared and prayed against like fire and lightning. I never asked why men raped; I simply thought it one of the many mysteries of human nature. (Griffin, 1971:26)

[2] Ms. Griffin is an active participant in the feminist movement. She holds no specialized degree in criminology, but her analysis of rape is considerably richer than standard works on the subject by academic criminologists.

She describes how her grandmother warned her to beware of strange men who might want to hurt her. Later that year a schoolmate tried to rape her.

Despite the ever-present reality of rape, one finds that little has been written about the subject. Many of the popular theories of rape are in fact myths. For example, we are led to believe that rapists are mentally deranged, but according to criminologist Menachem Amir (1971), almost all rape offenders appear to be psychologically normal. We also hear the theory (Amir, 1971) that rape is an impulsive act natural to most men, but in fact most rapes are planned. Other rape myths suggest that every woman has a secret desire to be raped or that rape is impossible if the victim tries to resist.

Switching the analysis to public issues, Ms. Griffin shows that sex and violence are often linked in our culture. In her view, the erotic pleasure of the male is wedded to power, and power is culturally defined as the unity of sex and violence. Males are taught to exploit women aggressively, and they are taught that women should be docile and yielding. Evidence from accounts of group rape suggests that the presence of other men tended to increase sadism and even cause the multiple rapes. "Thus it becomes clear that not only does our culture teach men the rudiments of rape, but society, or more specifically, other men, encourage the practice of it." (*Ibid.*, p. 30)

The other side of the cultural image of rape is the expectation that the male will protect his woman. As part of this sexual bargain, the woman must submit to the cultural expectations of chastity, virginity, and monogamy. It is assumed that the woman who does not conform to this sexual double standard *asks for rape.* This last aspect of the culture of rape is best exemplified by the treatment by police and court officials of the woman who is raped. Police often attempt to interrogate the victim about the exact details of the sexual assault.

> A woman who was raped in Berkeley was asked to tell the story of her rape four different times "right out in the street," while her assailant was escaping. She was then required to submit to a pelvic examination to prove that penetration had taken place. Later, she was taken to the police station where she was asked the same questions again: "Were you forced?" "Did he penetrate?" "Are you sure your life was in danger and you had no other choice?" This woman had been pulled off the street by a man who held a 10-inch knife to her throat and forcibly raped her. She was raped at midnight and was not able to return to her home until five in the morning. Police contacted her twice again in the next week, once by telephone at two in the morning and once at four in the morning. (*Ibid.*, p. 32)

Later, the victim described above recalled that "the rape was probably the least traumatic incident of the whole evening. If I'm ever raped again . . . I wouldn't report it to the police because of all the degradation. . . ." *(Ibid.)*

The treatment of third-world women who are victims of rape is often more offensive than that described above. The third-world woman confronts the mix of racist and sexist attitudes that define her as impure from birth and therefore free to be raped.[3]

Ms. Griffin next looks at legal codes to find an explanation for the personal troubles of the rape victim. She finds that the legal proscription against rape reflects "a possessory view of women." A prominent legal authority on rape laws has concluded that the basic rationale behind such laws was to provide an orderly outlet for the vengeance of the man whose privilege of bodily access had been violated. In no state can a man be accused of raping his wife. Rape laws enforce the conception of women as property and essentially protect one man's property against others.

Later in her article Ms. Griffin explains that inter-racial rape is largely a device by which white males subjugate persons of color. On one hand, the black woman is open to rape by the white oppressor; on the other, the myth of white womanhood is used as a war cry to justify the lynching of black men.

> Indeed, the existence of rape in any form is beneficial to the ruling class of white males. For rape is a kind of terrorism which severely limits the freedom of women and makes them dependent upon men. Moreover, in the act of rape, the rage that one man may harbor toward another higher in the male hierarchy can be deflected toward the female scapegoat. For every man there is always someone lower on the social scale on whom he can take out his aggressions. And that is any woman alive. . . . Rape is not an isolated act that can be rooted out of the patriarchy without ending the patriarchy itself. (*Ibid.*, 34)

A Garrison State in a "Democratic Society"

Paul Takagi's study of killings involving police and citizens is another illustration of the translation of personal troubles of milieu (policemen and citizens killing one another) to public issues (the role

[3] See, for example, Margaret Walker's historical novel, *Jubilee* (1969).

of police in American society). He begins by discussing FBI statistics that appear to show police officers being assassinated at an alarming rate. In 1971, 125 police officers were killed, an increase of more than 125 percent over 1963, when 55 officers were killed. Takagi points out a contradiction in that news accounts have underscored this apparent rise in police killings, whereas police killings of citizens are hardly ever reported as a problem of national scope. Rather, the latter tend to be reported as isolated events. Typically, the rise in the killing of police is reported as "unprecedented," and the rising political militancy of revolutionary groups is offered as an explanation by the media. Takagi explains that political officials have portrayed this problem as essentially one of military defense. Viewed as a military problem, the killing of police provides one justification for massive fortification of police weaponry through LEAA (Law Enforcement Assistance Administration) funding (Goulden, 1970).

Takagi shows that although the absolute number of policemen killed has increased, the rate of killings per active officers has not increased because of the tremendous rise in the number of sworn officers during the period 1963–71. This finding is consistent with a number of earlier studies that have shown the rate of police killed to be fairly constant over time. Data from the California Bureau of Criminal Statistics show that "ambushing" of police is relatively rare, accounting for only 25 percent of the police killed in 1970. Most officers die while conducting routine investigations, responding to disturbance calls, and taking persons into custody. If we include accidental deaths of police officers among the number of police killed, we discover that, contrary to the popular view, police work is not the most hazardous profession. Data compiled by Robin indicate that a number of other occupations have a higher fatality rate. The table on page 10 shows this relative occupational hazard.

The table shows that employees in the mining industry experienced an occupational death rate nearly three times that of law enforcement officers. Moreover, three of the other occupations were also found to be more dangerous than police work. Although it may be argued that police deaths are more frightening because they are calculated, Robin's data destroy the myth that police work is especially dangerous. Indeed, deaths in other occupations exhibit a frightening calculable regularity, but the fatality rate in these areas has not yet justified massive changes in the work situation.

Takagi adds an important new dimension to the issue of police killed by presenting data on the other side of the picture—citizens

Occupational Fatalities per 100,000 Employees—1955[a]

Occupation	*Fatality Rate per 100,000*
Mining	93.58
Construction Industry	75.81
Agriculture	54.97
Transportation	44.08
Law Enforcement	32.76
Public Utilities	14.98
Finance, Gov. Service	14.18
Manufacturing	12.08
Trade	10.25

[a]Adapted by Takagi from Robin and presented in Takagi, 1974, p. 28.

killed by police. These data are rather hard to come by and are virtually ignored in criminological research: "For example, the prestigious President's *Task Force Report* on the police (1967) devotes not one line to this issue" (Takagi, 1974:29). The number of citizens killed by police (or, in official terms, "by legal intervention by the police") can be dug out of *Vital Statistics in the United States*, an annually published compendium of data on births and deaths. Appearing under the undramatic heading of "Causes of Death, Code 984," these data do tell a dramatic story.

From 1962 to 1968 (the last year of available national statistics) there was a steady increase in the number and rate of male citizens over ten years of age who were killed by police action. In California the rate of civilians killed by police increased by 150 percent between 1962 and 1969.

> This increase cannot be attributed simply to an increase in the number of young adults in the population, among whom a larger share of these deaths occur, because each annual rate is age-adjusted to the age-profile of the population in 1960. There is an increase in the rate of homicides by police, regardless of changes in that age profile. (*Ibid.*)

Takagi explores the possibility that by committing more crimes, more males are placing themselves in a position to be killed. But he rejects this hypothesis as too simplistic, focusing the sole blame on the victim. The increased crime rate during the period 1962–68 did not result in an increase in the rate of policemen killed. "The point . . . is inescapable: the rate of death did not change for law enforcement officers during a period when it changed critically for male citizens." (*Ibid.*)

More startling than the above finding are Takagi's data showing that in California between nine and ten times more black men were killed than white men. During the years 1960–69 police killed 1,188 black males, compared with 1,253 white males; and this in a population where whites outnumber blacks by more than ten to one. Can this statistic be explained by the higher involvement of blacks in crime? Takagi answers no. For example, in 1964 black males accounted for 28 percent of all arrests, but in the same year blacks constituted 51 percent of those killed by policemen. In 1968 the statistical picture remained essentially the same. The percentage of blacks killed by police exceeded the percentage of blacks participating in violent crimes. To dramatize this racial discrepancy, Takagi presents data about quite old or very young citizens killed by police. The argument is that persons in these age groups are not likely to be "desperate" criminals. The following table presents these data from 1964 to 1968.

Rate of Death by Police Intervention—per Million/Yearly[a]

	Number		Rates	
	White	*Black*	*White*	*Black*
Ages 10 to 14	5	11	0.12	1.75
Ages 65 and over	5	14	0.14	4.76

[a]Adapted from Takagi, 1974, p. 30.

"In proportion to population, Black youngsters and old men have been killed by the police at a rate 15 to 30 times greater than for whites of the same age. It is the actual experiences behind statistics like these that suggest the police have one trigger finger for whites and another for Blacks." (*Ibid.*, p. 30)

Black citizens have often claimed that the killing of citizens by police is tantamount to genocide against blacks. Police are rarely held culpable in these killings. A Chicago study by Knoohuizen et al. (1972) provides anecdotal evidence that police are murdering citizens. The authors cite several cases in which the officer was held blameless but in which the facts speak otherwise. Here is one such case.

> The victim was Linda Anderson. Police action resulting in her death was ruled justifiable homicide because, according to police reports, she was killed accidentally during an attempt to gain access to her apartment by

> shooting the lock off the door. The partner of the officer, and independent witnesses, corroborated the police officer's version. An independent investigation revealed that the officer used a shotgun [and was] standing four feet from the door, did not warn the occupant of [the] impending shot, and missed the lock completely. (Knoohuizen et al., 1972:61)

Knoohuizen et al. found that in 28 of the 76 cases occurring in 1969–70 in which civilians were killed by Chicago police, there was substantial evidence of police misconduct; and in 10 of the 76 cases there was substantial evidence of criminal liability for manslaughter or murder. But only in extraordinary rare instances are policemen convicted, even if they are indicted by grand juries. Cases that do reach the court are usually thrown out, or a verdict of not guilty is rendered. Takagi cites a recent case in San Diego, California in which an officer shot a 16-year-old following a high-speed chase of an allegedly stolen car. The youth was unarmed, but the officer fired when he thought that the youth was reaching for his pocket. The judge dismissed the charges of involuntary manslaughter and added, "I think the officer deserves a commendation for doing his duty, rather than standing trial."

In another case, in San Antonio, Texas, a policeman shot a 12-year-old Mexican-American youngster who was under custody in a police car. The incident resulted from the officer's holding the barrel of his gun to the child's head and "playing Russian roulette." Takagi notes that "the circumstances in [this] case were so gross that a dismissal was out of the question. The court, however, sentenced the officer to a prison term of 5 years in a state where sentences of 1,000 years for lesser crimes are not uncommon." (Takagi, 1974:31)

The problem of protecting the lives of police officers has been defined by decision makers in terms of short term reforms. Solutions are usually suggested in terms of greater fortification, more security measures, or better community relations programs. A variety of proposals to curtail the use of deadly force by policemen have been made; these range from more stringent firearm regulations within police departments to psychological screening of police officers. Takagi notes that despite the proliferation of reforms, the toll of citizens killed by police persists. Perhaps the disarming of the police is the only short-term solution to the situation; of course, this proposal would be sharply opposed by police organizations. Increased alienation between the police and minority communities seems a more likely outcome.

To understand the problem—the killing of citizens by the police—one needs to relate it to the realm of public issues. Necessarily, this means considering the meaning of policing in contemporary America. Takagi argues that we need to understand the distinction between distributive justice and social justice. If the police officer who killed the alleged car thief were to be tried and convicted, this would be an example of distributive justice, in that the policeman would not have received special treatment by the courts. But the pursuit of social justice requires that one consider the reasons why the police officer resorted to deadly force in an auto theft case. In other words, "Why was the value of an automobile placed above the value of a human life?" (*Ibid.*, p. 32) The judge who said that the officer was only "doing his duty" tells us that the policeman's duty is first and foremost to protect private property; his legal responsibility was to protect the property rights of the automobile owner. Takagi analyzes this duty as follows.

> The critical issue here is that the auto theft laws and for that matter most laws in American society essentially legitimate a productive system where human labor is systematically expropriated. Examine for a moment the social significance of an automobile: it involves an array of corporate systems that expropriate the labor of people that go into the manufacture of its parts, the labor for its assembly, the labor involved in extracting and processing the fuel that propels it, the labor of constructing the roads on which it runs, etc. The fiction of ownership exacts further capital by banking institutions that mortgage the commodity, and automobile insurance required by laws that extorts further capital. The built-in obsolescence, or more precisely, the depreciation of the commodity occurs when the muscle, the sweat, and the human potential have been completely capitalized. These are the elements embodied in an automobile. It is no longer merely a commodity value, but represents a social value. (*Ibid.*)

The automobile is a commodity created out of several forms of wage labor. Following Marx, Takagi argues that the value of the automobile accrues through expropriated labor power. Thus, the concept of private ownership is based upon a form of wealth that depends upon the theft of labor power. Criminal laws and systems of law enforcement exist to promote and protect a system based upon this conception of property, and these laws and systems of organized violence or coercion are thus linked intimately with those persons who possess the most private property. In such a social structure laws provide a perverse justification for killing: to maintain the sanctity of property rather than life. This, for Takagi, is the meaning of policing in American society.

To explain the fact that blacks are killed ten times more frequently than whites, one must understand the workings of racism as well as the fact that institutional racism can itself yield surplus profits to those who control labor power. Urban ghettos provide a classic example of exploited labor, exploitation of tenants by slum landlords, and merchants selling inferior goods at high prices. Maintaining these conditions requires that regulatory agencies overlook the law, such as housing codes, labor laws, and food and drug regulations.

Takagi suggests that as blacks entered the competitive labor market, a variety of devices were required to continue their oppression. Presently, blacks find themselves among the continually unemployed, which may explain the increased number of blacks in prisons and the excessive violence used by law enforcement officials toward blacks. Takagi even goes so far as to suggest that the killing of blacks by police is a means of controlling a surplus labor population. Takagi's analysis does not answer all of the questions posed by the killing of civilians by police. Why do police in one city kill civilians at a higher rate than do police in another city? Why do police kill blacks at a disproportionately higher rate in cities such as Boston and Milwaukee? Why do the highly professionalized police in California kill citizens at a rate 60 percent higher than the national average?

Despite such unresolved questions, certain facts are clear. The most prominent of these facts is that the number of sworn police officers is growing at a much faster rate than our population. If current trends were to continue, there would be roughly 180,000 police officers in California by the year 2000. "Is it not true that the growth in the instruments of coercion and punishment is the inevitable consequence of the wealth of a nation that is based upon theft?" (*Ibid.*, p. 33)

"America," we are warned, "is moving towards a garrison state, and soon we will not find solace by repeating to ourselves: 'Ours is a democratic society' " (*Ibid.*). From the personal-problem level of the killing of civilians by police, to the public issue of an emerging garrison state—this is the sociological imagination applied to criminology.

Confronting the "Old" Criminology

One problem with conventional criminology is the general absence of historical insights in its theories. The student of criminology is presented with a history of sorts that upon scrutiny proves to be misleading, at best. Historical studies that can be found in early American criminology were written primarily by persons who were intimately concerned with the control of crime. This tradition of history written by persons whom Platt calls "scholar-technicians" is dominated by managers and spokesmen for the criminal justice system. The picture presented is of a steady march of enlightenment and reform. Almost never is this history related to sociopolitical events occurring at the time. Historical accounts of the development of social control agencies are usually descriptive, with little or no emphasis placed upon analysis and theory building.

Fortunately, adherents of the New Criminology are beginning to fill the gaps in our understanding of the history of crime and systems of social control. Perhaps the best known of these efforts is Anthony Platt's study of the origins of the Juvenile Court, *The Child Savers* (1969). Other examples are Ronald Boostrom's study of the emergence of American criminology (1974), Elliott Currie's work on the reformatory movement (1974), Gene Carte's biography of police reformer August Vollmer (1973), and Gregg Barak's study of the origins of the public defender movement (1974). As this historical research continues to flourish, it may give us many clues to the dynamics that propel current systems of social control.

We have learned from the studies cited above that the Progressive era (roughly 1880–1920) was a critical period in that most of what we think of as the modern criminal justice system was created during this time. We are led to conclude that most of the reforms developed in this period were designed to restore social order for a wealthy white establishment that felt threatened by labor strife, urban disorder, and the possibility of its own extinction. The reform effort was designed to strengthen the existing social structure through the introduction of rational and scientific means of controlling the "dangerous classes." From this historical perspective, the oppression of blacks, women, children, and political activists by the criminal justice system in modern America can be understood and analyzed. But serious gaps remain in our knowledge of the history of crime and social control. We still know relatively little about the development of the police. We have no accurate accounts of the treatment of blacks in Southern prison systems, nor do we as yet have a thorough understanding of the political, social, and economic factors that gave rise to social-control strategies and institutions.

Critics of the "Old" Criminology have commented on how that

field has prostituted itself in serving law enforcement and criminal justice agencies. Criminological theory has fostered and disseminated the hegemonic concepts of the ruling class, and empirical criminological studies have often supplied the technology of social control that has been employed in both domestic and foreign spheres.[4] Millions of dollars poured into criminological research by the Safe Streets and Omnibus Crime Control Act of 1967 through the LEAA have created an army of researchers who are attempting to introduce more "sophisticated" statistical techniques into court management, offender information systems, and predictions of delinquency, as well as mathematical models of riot control. Some criminologists have merged their role of researcher with the role of government consultant. And as Marvin Wolfgang has observed, when the criminologist is asked to join the "societal therapy team," he is likely to promote theories consistent with the views of those in power.

Much of the modern core of criminology was generated between 1880 and 1920—the same period that produced most of the elements of the modern criminal justice system. As new tests and research instruments were developed during these years, they were quickly applied to the study and classification of prisoners. Leading penologists of the age, such as Zebulon Brockway, celebrated the new scientific approach to prison management. Developing concepts such as mental inferiority and mental disease were used to explain criminal behavior. Criminal justice reformers hoped that more of the law would reflect scientific principles and that agencies of criminal justice would be run by principles of scientific management. One might speculate that the utility of the new science of criminology during this period of grave social conflict was to appear to depoliticize law enforcement in a period of intense political activity. The emergence of imperialism and the welfare state during this era of American history required the development of sociopolitical as well as military forms of domination. During this period influential persons in government and business rewarded social scientists, and in turn the social scientists masked their political ideology by claiming to be "neutral." The overall goal of most social scientists during this period was to replace a laissez-faire system of social control with a rational strategy of containing the threats posed by blacks, immigrants, the poor, and other members of the "dangerous classes."

[4] See the work of Janowitz (1968) on the control of riots, and that of Schwitzgebel (1971) on the use of electronic devices to track parolees.

One group of social scientists, whom I shall call "hip sociologists," have attempted to develop a point of view in which they reject "neutrality" and claim to side with "underdogs." These "hipsters," such as Howard Becker, Bennett Berger, and Erving Goffman, tell us that life is no more than a set of appearances. In this world of appearances all is leveled, including the hierarchy of values—which is, after all, what motivates political struggle. Those who can see through the world of everyday life can triumph as the cynical, liberal defenders of the underdog. Gouldner argues that the hipsters' criticism is directed at those who work for the "caretaking institutions" rather than at the powers that create the conditions of the deviant's suffering. The sociology of the underdog "succeeds in solving the oldest problem in personal politics: how to maintain one's integrity without sacrificing one's career, or how to remain a liberal although well heeled" (Gouldner, 1968:113).

Gouldner's criticism of the work of Erving Goffman is less personal and more profoundly political. Goffman's study of deviance represents for Gouldner the institutionalization of cynicism.[5] The actors in Goffman's world *make out,* or see only the level of personal troubles. Theirs is an individual and limited protest, which does not challenge the existing sociopolitical order but merely gives the illusion that they have beat the system by debunking it.

Other critics of the underdog perspective, such as Platt (1973) and Liazos (1972), have argued that analysis by this school continues to focus upon the individual deviant and his milieu.

> Close examination reveals that the writers of this field still do not try to relate the phenomenon of "deviance" to larger historical, political, and economic contexts. The emphasis is still on the "deviant" and the "problems" *he* presents to himself and others, not on the society within which he operates and emerges. (Liazos, 1972:104)

Liazos feels that by emphasizing the dramatic nature of a usual type of deviant behavior, such as mental illness, prostitution, or homosexuality, the hipsters deflect attention from more serious and harmful forms of "deviance."

> I refer to *covert institutionalized violence* which leads to such things as poverty and exploitation, the war in Viet Nam, unjust tax laws, racism and sexism, and so on, which cause psychic and material suffering for many Americans, black and white, men and women. (*Ibid.*)

[5] Sheldon Messinger et al. (1962) argue that this is a misinterpretation of Goffman's work.

Platt contends that

> while the labelling and conflict theorists, like Skolnick or Turk, are critical of social control institutions, their policy proposals are invariably formulated within the framework of corporate capitalism and the welfare state, and in effect help to shape new adjustments to existing political and economic arrangements. (Platt, 1973:4)

Liberal practicality in conventional criminology is also expressed in the notion of multiplicity of causes. Since there are so many causes of a problem, no one solution is feasible; rather, a group of possible solutions must be evaluated. Piecemeal reform efforts, when applied to social issues such as crime, racism, poverty, or mental illness, support the myth that progress and improvement can occur without major restructuring of the social order. A solution in terms of the redistribution of societal resources or in terms of self-determination is not permissible by liberal standards and is often rejected as impractical.[6] The standards of practicality are always taken from those who rule and who wish *to preserve their status quo*.

The ideology of criminologists is further revealed by their concept of adjustment. This concept may take on either a personal or a group meaning, but in either case criminality or delinquency is always located in the individual's immediate milieu. Various theories conclude that the solution for the deviant or the criminal, the impoverished or the mentally ill, is their successful integration into the mainstream of society. Likewise, the solution for racial and ethnic groups is assimilation and integration. Criminologists may cynically admit that structural inequities exist, but their paternalistic advice offered to the poor, people of color, women, and the young is to adjust, play within the system, appeal through "normal channels," and hope for the best. This message is *practical* in terms of the interests of those who gather privilege by exploiting others. Fortunately, many of the oppressed are beginning to conceive of *practical social changes that link individual success to the fate of the group*. In the interim some criminologists will serve as State apologists and issue justifications for the "benign neglect" of our most burning social issues.

One could point out many other deficiencies of the traditional criminological literature. Indeed, as we mentioned earlier, many of the adherents of the New Criminology are providing us with valuable insights by reanalyzing the work of the old masters. We would not go

[6] See William Ryan (1971).

so far as to advocate the blanket rejection of the older criminology; such a blanket rejection is as wrong as an uncritical acceptance of conventional criminology. There does exist, in that older literature, data that must be interpreted from the perspectives of the New Criminology. But we also need new sorts of data, and some of these data can be obtained only through the participation of New Criminologists in the "public issues of social structure."

To position oneself in the world of public issues and to apply this experience to the New Criminology is a demanding requirement of the sociological imagination. For some, especially those from oppressed groups, there is little choice in the matter; their fate is related to the fate of their fellows by history and by the current privilege structure. Perhaps by infusing the sociological imagination into the New Criminology, we may escape the mental prisons that Marie Bertrand spoke of. But the success of the sociological imagination is intimately related to the struggles of oppressed people for equality, self-determination, and social justice, because these are the groups that are actively seeking liberation, intellectually and politically. To stand for the sociological imagination is not a fashion or an aesthetic choice: ultimately, it commits one to social change.

TWO

Crime and Privilege

All criminals are victims of the attempt to maintain hierarchy. Any other conclusion denies original innocence, or in effect advances that men are criminals before they are born.

George Jackson, 1971.

To locate the study of crime within the broader quest for social justice demands that one understand the relationship of crime to the maintenance of privilege. The dynamics of crime can be understood within the context of the structures of injustice that are created by the powerful to further their domination. The concept of crime, as usually presented, serves to deflect attention from the violence and social damage that those with power inflict upon the mass of people in order to keep them subordinate and oppressed. In this chapter we will attempt to introduce concepts that unmask this relationship and provide a better perspective with which to understand how personal troubles relate to crime and crime control.

Privilege may be defined as the possession of that which is valued by a particular social group in a given historical period. Elements of privilege may include prerogatives such as the right to "life, liberty, and the pursuit of happiness"; culturally defined positive traits such as intelligence, sensitivity, religious salvation, or humanity; or specific material commodities that are culturally defined as valuable, such as property, monetary wealth, machines, or cultural artifacts. The system of privilege of a specific cultural group includes the rules by which the valued entities are distributed and the societal institutions that organize the distributive process. The structure of domination describes the group that defines what is to be valued and that controls entrance and access to the institutions distributing privilege. Force, the effective use of violence and coercion, is the major factor in determining which social group ascends to the position of defining and holding privilege.

Many theories seek to explain the origins and the dynamics of privilege. According to one writer, "Virtually all the major theorists in this field, regardless of their ideological biases, have sought to answer one basic question: *Who gets what and why?*" (Gerhard Lenski, in Rainwater, 1974:53) Marx for example, believed that the privilege structure—or, in his terms, class structure—was a product of the historical development of the mode of production. Indeed, history was the story of one class struggle after another. Marx saw the bourgeois class as bringing about the most recent revolution in the mode of production, which, in turn, created the seeds of class strife that would lead to the next revolutionary organization of society. The defining characteristic of class for Marx was relationship to the means of production: those who owned productive capital controlled society; those who were merely wage earners were the exploited under class.

The German sociologist Max Weber held a similar view: class relations were the product of historical change; but he was less sanguine about the possibility of class struggle as a history-making force. He agreed with Marx that ownership of the means of production was the crucial definer of class status. Weber observed, "The propertyless class of antiquity and of the Middle Ages protested against monopolies, pre-emption, forestalling, and withholding goods from the market in order to raise prices. Today the central issue is to determine the price of labor." (Weber, in Gerth and Mills, 1967:186) But whereas Marx believed that changes in the material economy produced changes in culture and social structure, Weber held the contrary viewpoint. In *The Protestant Ethic and the Spirit of Capitalism,* Weber argued that the distinctive cultural elements of the "Protestant ethic" produced the necessary condition for the growth of the economic structure of capitalism.

Marx tended to reduce all aspects of privilege to economically derived facts. He believed that categories such as race, sex, or nationality were products of civil society and that these distinctions would disappear with the growth of class consciousness. Weber, on the other hand, separated privilege into class, status, and power.

Classes, in Weber's view, are groups of people who share common life opportunities; these are based exclusively upon the possession of goods and opportunities for income. Classes are specific to commodity or labor markets. The key element in class is the ownership of property that can be successfully exploited by the owner in the market situation. Those whose fate is not determined by the opportunity to use goods or services for themselves on the market (slaves, for instance) are not a class but rather a *status group.* The culture provides the standards by which honor can be assessed. The primary expression of status is life style. One demonstrates through patterns of social interaction, publicly avowed belief systems, and consumption patterns, among other means, that one is of a particular status group. Status depends upon what Weber called "usurpation," the imposition of one set of standards on all of the society. Status arrangements are translated into legal privilege when "a certain stratification of the social order has been 'lived in' and has achieved stability by virtue of a stable distribution of economic power" (*Ibid.,* p. 188). The process of status differentiation reaches its logical outcome when a status group evolves into a *closed caste.* This is accomplished and guaranteed by conventions, laws, and a variety of rituals. Colonial situations are ideal for the solidification of status into caste. In these situations laws and common norms define the superiority of the colonist relative to the native, but the normative order is constantly reenforced by social rituals designed to demonstrate the divisions between colonist and native, master and slave.

Weber defined power as "the chance of a man or of a number of men to realize their own will against the resistance of others who are participating in the action" (*Ibid.,* p. 180). The organization of power into rationally planned collectivities is the origin of parties or interest groups. Weber argued that the structure of parties is determined largely by the structure of domination within the community, because parties deal with the conquest of the community. Parties are also derived from arrangements of status and class within the community.

The three closely interrelated aspects of privilege—class, status, and power—may be used to understand several of the anomalies of crime and justice. Consider the recent wave of prison riots that have resulted from intensive organizational efforts primarily from inside the walls.[1] In almost every case, prisoners define their role as laborers without

[1] John Pallas and Bob Barber (1972) provide an excellent summary of the growth of the prison movement and its major issues.

proper compensation or protection. They point to minuscule wages, the use of inmate welfare funds to support treatment programs, and the lack of accident insurance or adequate health care. Strikes at prisons such as Folsom and San Quentin in California embodied grievances against an unjust work and labor situation, as well as other injustices of the prison system. Groups such as the California Prisoners Union have charged that length of sentence is determined by the willingness of the inmate to participate in the camps and factories of the California Correctional Industries and the California Department of Forestry. They further assert that prisoners are *dehumanized* by slave wages of $.04 to $.16 an hour.

Prisoners' economic grievances are often coupled with protests against the denial to them of the rudimentary rights of civilians in the outside society. Prisoners charge that they are subject to invasion of privacy, brutalizing and inhuman treatment by guards, and conditions of custody designed to degrade them. Seeing themselves as a status group faced with legal proscriptions and a daily round of "status degradation ceremonies," prisoners have focused their rebellion on the conditions they consider demeaning. Many speak explicitly about their status as convicts in terms of a loss of honor relative to the free community. Prisoners are not to be trusted, not to be associated with, and presumed to be *less than human.* A constant prison ritual reinforces such status conceptions.

Power plays a central role in prisoner disputes. This can be seen in the universal rejection by prisoners and ex-prisoner groups of the indeterminate sentence law, which allows some administrative body, such as a state department of corrections or an adult corrections authority, to fix prison terms within limits broadly defined by law. Prisoners argue that this type of sentencing structure gives the sentencing body complete authority to make decisions concerning release on often irrelevant or unfair grounds. For example, the paroling authority may choose to deny parole not on the basis of the person's adjustment in prison or the facts of the current offense, but, instead, on the basis of some offense deep in the person's past.

Parole boards are particularly reluctant to parole individuals whom they define as racial militants. Being labeled a troublemaker in today's prison generally means that you are accused of being involved in some effort to organize prisoners as a political entity in order that they may protest the conditions of their imprisonment. That one reads "revolutionary" books or receives magazines such as *Mohammed Speaks* or *The Black Panther* is taken as prima-facie evidence that the prisoner is violent or potentially dangerous and thus should not be released. Such reading material is often confiscated or outlawed in the interests of "order" in the prison. Moreover, one of the conditions of parole is that the ex-prisoner may not associate with known felons, and this limits the organizing efforts of ex-offender groups.

Viewed from the perspective of class, status, and power, the recent prisoner riots can be interpreted as fundamental challenges to the privilege system imposed upon inmates by correctional systems. Further, prisoners relate the enforcement of privilege within the penal institution to the structure of privilege outside the walls. Some believe that by breaking the law they symbolize resistance to the oppression of the larger privilege system. This resistance, both symbolic and real, uncovers for them the reasons for the horrid conditions in prisons, the denial of legal rights to prisoners, and the use of deadly force to quell prisoner resistance inside the walls. The slaughter of rebellious prisoners in the prison at Attica, New York is a striking example of the use of force to protect and maintain the prison's order of privilege.

Another example of the workings of privilege in the criminal justice system may be seen in the career of a person going through the court system. Statistical studies as well as observations of the justice system demonstrate that the poor and third-world groups are most likely to be considered suspicious persons by police and are more subject to arrest. Police decision making is loaded heavily with class and status considerations.[2] Once arrested, the person without a job or without monetary resources is likely to be held over for trial and sent to jail because he or she does not have the money to make bail. Even in jurisdictions that have special release projects in lieu of arrest, such as release on own recognizance or a citations system, persons are screened for these alternatives by criteria such as length of employment, family stability, standing in the community, and so on. Class position determines that one can afford a private attorney or that one must accept a court-appointed public defender. It is well known that public defenders encourage defendants to plead guilty to one charge in exchange for having several charges dropped or reduced in seriousness. This is often rationalized by attorneys and judges as a way to promote efficiency and reduce court expenses. The defendant who enjoys a positive-defined social status, who is seen as a *respected member of the community,* is more likely to have all charges dropped or is more

[2] See Irving Piliavin and Scott Briar (1964); Marvin Wolfgang et al. (1972); and Jerome Skolnick (1966).

likely to be able to afford a costly jury trial, in which he has a better chance of being found not guilty. Privileged defendants can retain experienced trial lawyers and can pay for private investigation services or the testimony of expert witnesses, both of which may play a significant role in the finding of guilt or innocence. Similarly, most judges and juries enjoy positions of relative privilege and are more likely to believe the testimony of those who are close to them in class position or status.[3]

If the defendant is found guilty of a crime, class and economic variables largely determine the severity of the sentence given by the court. For example, the businessman indicted for tax evasion or embezzlement is likely to be merely fined, given a suspended sentence, or placed on probation; poor defendants, and third-world persons in particular, are sent to jail or prison for crimes that involve considerably less social harm. The convicted felon who can afford private psychiatric treatment is released to seek help; the impoverished convicted person is placed in prison to receive little or no professional help. Once incarcerated, the prisoner's ability to find a job, the stability of his family relations, and his acceptance of the authority of the state are used to determine his readiness for release.

In all phases of the legal process economic resources, access to resources of power such as private attorneys or influential friends, and the socially defined status of the defendant structure the chances that the individual will receive a fair trial or be treated justly by the court system. Such inequities cannot be explained as the sole result of the discretion of the police, prosecutors, or judges. That systematic injustices are meted out by the legal process suggests that the structural differences of privilege in the society circumscribe the operations of the criminal justice system. Virtually all tests, criteria, and classification instruments used in the criminal justice decision-making process are laden with class and racial bias.

Although it is seldom reported, women who are caught up in the criminal justice system are often subjected to harsher conditions than men.[4] They are likely to be treated with disrespect and brutality by police and correctional officers. Women's prisons are usually in worse condition than male facilities and have virtually no rehabilitation programs. In the few states that offer job training to male felons, women are trained for vocations such as laundry, domestic service,

[3] A fine case study is that of Peter Goldman and Dan Holt (1971).

[4] Jessica Mitford (1973) "Women in Cages" in *Kind and Unusual Punishment*; and Kitsi Burkhart (1971).

and sewing. In several states women who have children while in state custody are forced to put their children up for adoption. The fact that women are arrested less frequently than men does not suggest that they are treated more leniently, but rather that society has developed other, less costly means of keeping women subservient to men.[5]

The Dynamics of Privilege

Describing the process of domination in a given society is a difficult task because the available social theory tends to dismiss the existence of privilege. The task is further complicated by the absence of a clear-cut alternative social structure, in theory or in reality, for comparison. Moreover, the dynamics of particular privilege systems, such as racism, sexism, or class oppression, have distinct although similar patterns. Thus, it is nearly impossible to speak of one overall process of domination. The interconnections among systems of privilege remains a crucial area of theory for the New Criminology, and we are likely to spend a good deal of time in the future unraveling these interrelationships in pursuit of strategies of action.

For purposes of illustration, let us consider one view of the origin and dynamics of race privilege in America. With this model one can view the structure of other systems of domination in terms of similarities and distinctive qualities. This model of race privilege is taken from the work of sociologist Robert Blauner (1972).

Blauner explicitly uses the model of colonialism to describe the contours of race privilege in America. Many theorists of colonialism, such as Albert Memmi (1967) and Franz Fanon (1968), have argued that the essence of the colonial relationship is the preservation of the colonist's privilege. In Blauner's words, "The various forms of social oppression all involve exploitation and control. To generate privilege, certain people have to be exploited, and to be exploited they must be controlled—directly and indirectly." (Blauner, 1972:22) The mechanisms of control include violence and force, legal restrictions, cultural beliefs, and modes of socioeconomic integration. The dynamic process involves those actions used by the dominant group to foster their privilege and power; this they do by imposing burdens upon the persons defined as inferior. The oppressed are pushed lower and lower in the social order.

[5] This point is discussed by June Kress et al., "Women, Crime and Criminology" *Issues in Criminology* (Fall, 1973).

In a race privilege system, the dominant group thinks of itself as superior in terms of racial and ethnic differences. These distinctions can be real or socially constructed. Class systems define superiority in terms of the criteria relevant to control of the techno-economy, such as ownership of property, positions of economic power, and expertise in production. Systems of sex privilege make distinctions based upon gender, defining, in our society, male qualities as dominant and female characteristics as evidence of inferiority. Blauner argues that it does not matter whether racist or other practices are followed consciously or unconsciously to benefit the privileged. All practices that buttress the system of domination benefit those who hold the "desirable" qualities. Privilege systems render particular groups "unfair advantage, a preferential situation, or a systematic 'headstart' in pursuit of social values" *(Ibid.)*. Inequalities are built into stratified societies, even those that do not exhibit sharp distinctions based upon race and ethnicity. But when injustices and inequities fall most heavily upon persons of color and the principles used to justify privilege are guided by differences of race or ethnicity, such a society is racist in addition to the other characteristics of its stratification.

Privileges usually extend to all aspects of social life. In America one observes the workings of race privilege from cradle to grave. Despite its affluence, our society has one of the highest rates of infant mortality in the industrialized world. Oppressed racial groups have a shorter life expectancy than whites and exhibit higher death rates from almost every form of disease.[6] Death by suicide, drug overdose, or violence is the special fate of persons of color in this country. Inadequate medical care and the overburdening pressures of their everyday life contribute to the premature aging of the racially oppressed.

Race privilege is observed in all areas of our existence. Housing, quality of neighborhood environment, education, income, and diet are all defined by race privilege. Race distinctions are greatest in terms of life opportunities and the quality of existence. Furthermore, these differences are enforced *within* the dominant white group, to the detriment of the economically downtrodden and women. In a racist society, certain characteristics of race privilege are also seen in the oppression of women and the poor. According to Blauner, race privileges cannot be avoided.

> The children of the middle class who have "dropped out" to live in near-poverty conditions always reserve their racial privileges when and if

[6] See William Ryan (1971: 155–63).

> they decide to reenter the mainstream. . . . And from the civil rights movement to the more recent student demonstrations, the white radicals have received relatively more benign treatment from the police and the courts than their third world counterparts. (*Ibid.*, p. 23)

Race privileges operate in all major institutions of the social structure and are particularly expressed in the economic system, which in an industrial, capitalist society is central to the determination of social status and life style. Blauner believes that the advantage of the white population in the labor market is especially important in the maintenance of the systematic privilege that undergirds a racist, capitalist social order.

Third-world Americans are confined to the lowest stratum of the work force. They suffer continuous high rates of unemployment and underemployment. Some, for example, have argued that blacks have experienced a relatively stable rate of unemployment since the 1930s. In a provocative work, *Who Needs the Negro* (1970), Sidney Willhelm suggests that racism against blacks has always operated within the boundaries of the need of the capitalist system to exploit its labor supply. Wars have traditionally meant slightly better times for blacks in the labor force. But Willhelm asserts that automation has made Negro labor unnecessary, and the specter of unbridled race oppression thus seems imminent to him. Blauner believes that third-world workers fit Marx's conception of an industrial reserve army, which meets the system's needs for an elastic labor pool.

Oppressed racial groups are concentrated in jobs that are insecure, unskilled, and considered undesirable, and that offer little or no chance for advancement. On the other side, white workers have a monopoly or near monopoly on jobs "that are secure, clean, highly skilled, involve authority, and provide the possibilities of promotion" (Blauner, 1972:23). Certain jobs are seemingly reserved for persons of color. These include cleaning floors and toilets, shining shoes, cleaning up after the sick in hospitals, digging graves, and washing dishes. We can see here the parallel of job categories that are defined as "woman's work," such as domestic service, secretarial and typing jobs, and child care. Often, women and racial minorities are found together in industries such as clothing or food service. Generally, these jobs pay according to piecework rather than wage systems and exhibit the worst working conditions. Often, such occupations do not offer usual protections such as workman's compensation, retirement systems, health insurance, and unemployment insurance. Women, particularly those who enter the labor force in middle age, constitute another part of the reserve industrial army that Marx described. And among the exploited female labor supply, it is third-world women who suffer the worst in the job marketplace.

The labor force is a critical factor in the continuance of privilege: the unusually low wages given to third-world or women laborers means that a surplus of labor is exacted from them; eventually, this surplus labor results in profits or in further industrial development. Later, we will attempt to show that this "surplus value" of labor is central to the building of the capitalist industrial empire. The oppression of the third-world person in the job market provides another means by which the privileged class maintains its power: it provides the white working class with the mythology that they benefit from the system of industrial organization. White workers do benefit in a relative way: "The white working class elevates itself from the contamination of [certain kinds of] unpleasant work and in the bargain increases its share of 'good, clean jobs.' " (*Ibid.,* p. 24) Most labor unions have been powerful instruments by which the white working class insulates itself from the supposed threat of third-world workers. But the focus upon protecting the whiteness and the maleness of the skilled labor market has served the industrial elite by deflecting attention from issues of industrial justice and democracy. Limited gains by white workers may be compared with their psychological rewards relative to blacks and other racial groups, and the overall objectives of the ruling class are served by such a limited comparison of privilege. The process of white workers defining their superiority over third-world people parallels attempts by working-class whites to prevent contamination of their neighborhoods, churches, and schools by racially oppressed groups. In recent years, the dominant group appears to have become less resistant to third-world incursions upon their domains because they have used the white under classes to keep blacks and other groups from effective socioeconomic gains. Facts, however, disprove this seeming liberality of the privileged. Grosse Pointe is more of an all-white preserve than working-class areas in Detroit; likewise, Shaker Heights is the bastion of white privilege among the neighborhoods of Cleveland. Several studies demonstrate that racial exclusion varies directly with the money value of property in areas of almost every American city. It was the wealthy who led the flight from the increasingly black inner city and who protected their young from racial intermixing by placing them in expensive private schools. Middle- and working-class whites were permitted to "escape" to suburban areas abandoned by the privileged for more desirable settlements.

A recent study by Thurow (1969), based upon the 1960 census, lists the economic gain of whites during the 1950s as $15.5 billion, derived through five areas of racial discrimination: more steady employment, higher wages, more lucrative occupations, greater investment in human capital (education), and labor union monopoly. The same figures show third-world groups to enjoy only 50 to 60 percent of the income of whites. Racial discrepancies in income vary from society to society, according to Thurow. In colonial societies overseas, such as South Africa or prerevolutionary Algeria, the tiny ruling settler classes had between ten and twenty times as much income as the native populations. In our country comparable racial discrepancies in income are best seen by comparing plantation owners with slaves in the ante-bellum South and the upper classes with the poor in contemporary American society. As income differences are enforced according to racial or sexual criteria, most whites and males will benefit, but the most privileged will receive the greatest share of the rewards of oppression.

The stark differences in the distribution of material goods in advanced capitalist societies has led some to consider race privilege an artifact of economic injustices. But Blauner reminds us that "race privilege is not simply economic. It is a matter of status also." (Blauner, 1972:27) Systems of racial privilege are buttressed by the denial of social honor to third-world people. Cultural values of beauty, goodness, and humanity are cited to demonstrate the inferiority of oppressed races. Harsh systems of race oppression such as slavery or colonialism are filled with rituals designed to degrade and devalue the social worth of third-world peoples. The utter brutality of slave and colonial situations cannot be explained merely by economic referents. The cultural animosity of whites toward people of color is deeply imbedded in language. As Winthrop Jordan has observed, "Black was an emotionally partisan color, the handmaiden and symbol of baseness and evil, a sign of baseness and repulsion" (Jordan, 1974:6). Long before the development of capitalism the cultural meaning of blackness was filled with all the connotations of nonhuman things. Jordan notes that an edition of the *Oxford English Dictionary* published before the sixteenth century contained the following meaning of "black":

> Deeply stained with dirt; . . . soiled . . . , horrible, dirty, foul. . . . Having dark or deadly purposes, malignant; pertaining to or involving

> death; deadly; baneful, disastrous, sinister. . . . Foul, iniquitous, atrocious, horrible, wicked. . . . Indicating disgrace, censure, liability to punishment, etc. *(Ibid.)*

Note the obvious connections between the cultural meaning of blackness to whites and the concepts of crime and punishment. The determinants of color differences and the supposed differences between criminals and noncriminals are similar throughout most of white Euro-American history. Repeated attempts to discover the difference between whites and others in terms of religious or quasi-scientific criteria are almost identical with the attempts to describe the causes of criminality. Consider Lombroso's belief that criminals exhibited "Negroid" features, or more recent efforts to explain violence in terms of biological or psychological traits particular to criminals and members of "inferior" racial groups. A constant theme in racist ideology is the criminality of nonwhites and their threat to white civilization. From this perspective, it is not surprising to find that race is regarded as evidence of possible criminality by law enforcement officers, or that police are more likely to shoot blacks than whites, or that our prisons are becoming what some regard as racial concentration camps.

The American legal system has consistently upheld the superiority of white privilege. Consider the early Constitutional provision defining a black as three fifths of a man or the Supreme Court decision legalizing the internment of Japanese-Americans during World War Two (*Korematsu* v. *United States* (1944)). Legal support for oppressed groups has been rare and substantially without practical consequence for the lives of third world peoples in this country.[7] The white justice system has almost always meant broken treaties, the enforcement of white superiority, and the repression of third-world movements aimed at self-determination and the pursuit of social justice. It is significant that virtually every progressive leader of black people in this country has been imprisoned or assassinated—from Nat Turner to Martin Luther King, from Marcus Garvey to Dr. W. E. B. Du Bois. Members of all third-world groups know, all too well, that the justice of the legal institutions is for whites only. Blauner notes that the ability of white Europeans to command status in every racially mixed society on the basis of color alone is by far the most fateful example in history of the tendency of one group to maximize its social status at the expense of all others.

[7] Haywood Burns, "Racism and American Law", in Lefcourt (1971).

Blauner tells us that the predominance of race privilege throughout American history does not diminish the importance of class and sexual oppression in our society today. "Race affects class formation and class influences racial dynamics in ways that have not as yet been adequately investigated" (Blauner, 1972:29). The complexity of constructing a model with which to understand a racial, capitalist social structure is not merely a theoretical problem; a fundamental analysis of the interrelations of race, class, and sex is necessary in the work of community organizers and others who would launch social movements to challenge the social order.

The dynamics of racial oppression and, indeed, all forms of social injustice may be understood in the workings of exploitation and control. Europeans' expanding control during the fifteenth century began a process of conquest and exploitation that lingers to the present day. Conquest was generally followed by the establishment of a racial division of labor, such as the slave plantation, the hacienda of Indo-America, and, later, the colonization of Africa and Asia. Basic to the division of labor was the exploitation of the work of the colonized.

Marx has shown us that exploitation of labor is central to the colony as well as the factory. Such exploitation required discipline and control: "When unpleasant tasks are not integrated into kinship networks or traditional rituals, people have to be induced to do them for a minimal remuneration—especially when others determine the conditions of work and appropriate the results." *(Ibid.)* In *Capital,* Marx described the brutal and heavy-handed control exerted by the capitalist class over workers during the English industrial revolution. Blauner suggests that the problem of control and discipline is greater in the colonial context than in the factory system. Younger workers of the European proletariat did resist and attempted to organize against those who dominated them; this resulted in forms of industrial discipline designed to control the subversive aspects of such movements. After a protracted struggle in both Europe and the United States, working classes were given some privileges and rights, such as collective bargaining, shorter work hours, minimum wage laws, and limited access to political power through participation in the *established* political parties. But in general these concessions have served to strengthen rather than weaken the wealth and privilege of the capitalist class. The price for citizenship for the worker was that he give up the threat to the capitalist social structure. Industrial control was institutionalized in terms of collective bargaining and grievance procedures that, in the end, meant more predictable and thus more efficient exploitation of labor. Profits continued to soar as workers gained specific rights and privileges within the limited factory setting.

The problem of order in multiracial labor systems was considerably greater than that posed by white workers because the system of race privilege did not permit the granting of citizenship rights that were reserved for whites. The labor force was considered alien in cultural traditions. Physical coercion and violence played the major role in enforcing work discipline. And because the basis of the control was force, the possibility of resistance and revolt appeared great to the white exploiters. Jordan provides an excellent description of the "Anxious Oppressors", i.e., whites during slavery (Jordan, 1974:57–68). He shows that white slave owners were obsessed with fears of black insurrection and rebellion. They came to fear that all freed blacks were fomenting revolt, and they thus associated free black men with the threat of violence and death. This fear of slave revolt prompted constant reformulation of codes regulating slave behavior and the behavior of whites toward slaves.

The alien character of the colonized and the coercive nature of the labor system are united in the establishment of a race privilege system in which white supremacy per se comes to be valued: "Since the kind of citizenship that integrated workers into advanced capitalism was not a possibility, racial control became an end in itself, despite its original limited purpose as a means to exploitation and privilege." (Blauner, 1972:31)

Cultural domination is an integral part of the system of race privilege. Whites constructed elaborate ideologies to convince themselves that their oppression of third-world peoples was justified and to inculcate the oppressed with feelings of inferiority. People of color were assaulted with rituals, written history, education systems, and mass-media presentations that reinforced the cultural superiority of whites. Their own cultural contributions were ignored, downgraded, or absorbed by the privileged culture: "Even the promise of assimilation to those individuals whose adaptations were deemed successful was at bottom a control device, since assimilation weakened the communities of the oppressed and implicitly sanctioned the idea of white cultural superiority." (*Ibid.,* p. 32) The ultimate irony is that white social scientists have dominated the academic fields that describe and explain the "social problems" faced by third-world peoples. Furthermore, it is they who have helped develop the programs that are supposed to uplift the "disadvantaged." But by and large, these social theories and therapies deny that race privilege is a systematic feature of American life, and the "solutions" place the focus of the problem upon the oppressed themselves.[8]

Systems of race privilege depend, finally, upon control over the movements of the oppressed and the restriction of their full participation in society. This control may be secured through laws or by violence. Or it may be enforced through cultural domination and psychological oppression: "Here the notion of *place* is central. The idea that there is an appropriate place—or set of roles and activities—for people of color, and that other places and possibilities are not proper or acceptable is a universal element of the racist dynamic." (*Ibid.*, pp. 37–38) The place reserved for third-world people is always *less* than that set aside for whites. Thus, as Blauner observes, the essence of race privilege is to deny the individual or subjugated group the full range of human possibilities. Colonized people are converted, in the oppressor's mind, into objects to be used for the pleasure and profit of the colonizer. Stereotypes of persons of color are laden with imagery of them as children or animals, "the better to justify such less than human forms of relatedness" (*Ibid.*, p. 41). In this context it is easy to understand why "the explosion of creative talent and political leadership has emerged from the prisons and the streetcorners" (*Ibid.*, p. 40). Those who refuse to accept an inferior share of life will exhibit careers of school difficulties, brushes with the law, and rejection of the mainstream of American culture. This last observation is particularly crucial because it alerts us that systems of privilege help create their own opposition. Out of the violence and cultural suffocation visited upon oppressed peoples comes the creative and driving force that summons the masses to resist the structures of domination. Truth and time, asserted Malcolm X, are on the side of the oppressed.

The Criminality of the Privileged

"Behind every great fortune," wrote Balzac, "there is a crime." The rise of persons of great wealth in this country includes the story of relentless fraud, violence, and theft. The many tales of the criminality of the privileged, such as Gustavus Myers's *Story of Great American Fortunes*, Matthew Josephson's *The Robber Barons* (1934), and Stewart Holbrook's *The Age of the Moguls* (1953), led a noted expert on organized crime, Gus Tyler, to conclude that the evolution of

[8] See William Ryan's *Blaming the Victim* (1971) for a brilliant dissection of this form of ideological oppression.

organized crime in America recapitulates the history of western capitalism.

> Original accumulations of capital were amassed in tripartite deals among pirates, governors, and brokers. Fur fortunes were piled up alongside the drunk and dead bodies of our noble savages, the Indians. Small settlers were driven from their lands or turned into tenants by big ranchers, employing rustlers, guns, outlaws, and the law. In the great railroad and shipping wars, enterprising capitalists used extortion, blackmail, violence, bribery, and armies with muskets and cannons to wreck a competitor and to become the sole boss of the trade. (Tyler, 1962:44–45)

Tyler explains that the parallel between the growth of financial empires and of the criminal syndicate is remarkable. Both systems depend upon the ultimate containment of violence, running a peaceful and prudent business, and establishing law and order on its turf.

The career of J. Pierpont Morgan, one of the greatest of all American capitalists, reveals this familiar pattern. The Civil War provided Morgan with his first opportunity to make large amounts of money. A committee of the House of Representatives characterized one of his early transactions as "an effort to obtain from the government some $49,000 over and above the value of the property sold" and "a crime against the public safety" (quoted in Lewis Corey, 1930:57). The deal, which involved several parties, involved the attempt to resell to the U.S. Government armaments that had already been purchased and declared unfit for use. Morgan's role in the operation was that of broker and financier. Later in Corey's classic exposé of the Morgan empire, we are told how Morgan and his competitors hired bands of armed mercenaries to fight over the control of key railroad interests. One of Morgan's great abilities seems to have been bribing state legislatures and judges. The buying and selling of judicial officers, which resulted in the rendering of favorable court verdicts, was seen by many as almost completely discrediting the legal profession in New York State. Corey reports that many bankers were intimidated by the rough-and-tumble practices of industrialists such as Jay Gould and Jim Fisk (famous in their day for watering stock and for other fraudulent credit transactions); "but Morgan was not. He met force with force, guile with guile, methods which Morgan subsequently combined with the technique of using the concentrated power of massed money to conquer his objectives. The combination was irresistible." (*Ibid.*, p. 112)

Although the robber baron has been replaced by the "button-down" corporate executive, the pattern of crime by the privileged continues. We are often unaware of corporate criminality because of the elaborate legal resources that businessmen have to circumvent prosecution. Moreover, the court system recognizes the privileged position of the corporate criminal and tends to treat him with respect and a great deal of leniency. Long ago, criminologist Edwin Sutherland showed that white-collar criminals were treated specially by the criminal justice system. Sutherland concluded that laws against white-collar crimes such as price fixing, fraudulent advertising, violations of the Pure Food and Drug Act, and labor violations were structured to conceal the criminality of the behavior and that the enforcement of such laws was extremely ineffective. The criminal process in cases involving corporate criminals is increasingly being assumed by administrative rather than judicial bodies. Such administrative bodies as the Food and Drug Administration, the Federal Aeronautics Administration, the National Labor Relations Board, and the Antitrust Division of the Department of Justice are often controlled by persons favorable to industry; or these boards comprise representatives of the industries they are supposed to oversee.

Many corporate crimes are of such magnitude and complexity that they challenge experts to uncover wrongdoing. A case in point is the recent bankruptcy of the Penn Central Railroad. Initial reports about the manipulation of the railroad's financial statement showed that a substantial deficit was transformed into a misleading "paper" surplus. News reports assured readers that this fiscal statement, which was prepared by one of the most prestigious accounting firms in the country, was completed "according to sound accounting principles." Other allegations against the Penn Central management were that friends and financial associates were given advance notice of the impending demise of the company and that this enabled them to dump large quantities of worthless stock upon unsuspecting investors.

Other cases of corporate crime are less subtle, but the treatment by the courts of wrongdoers in even the most notorious cases is quite lenient. A price-fixing case involving virtually all the major electrical manufacturers in the United States produced forty-five defendants in a celebrated criminal trial (see Smith, 1961:132–80). A private reporter working for the Tennessee Valley Authority publicized the fact that sealed bids submitted to the TVA for the purchase of electrical equipment were identical down to the last decimal. Although corporate price fixing had been practiced in a number of industries, the difference in this case was the deliberate scheming and consultation among high executives to set prices on electrical goods. Their conspiracy involved secret meetings, code words, and elaborate plans to mask their activities. Although several of the indicted officials acknowledged their complicity in the conspiracy, most justified their actions in terms of "orders from higher ups" or by justifying their behavior as *standard business practice.* One defendant in the case observed, "No one attending the gatherings was so stupid that he didn't know that the meetings were in violation of the law. But it is the only way that a business can be run. It is free enterprise." (quoted in Fuller, 1962:91)

Quite recently, the press revealed a scandal involving the Equity Funding Corporation of America. This corporation, one of the largest American insurance-finance institutions, went bankrupt after the fraudulent practices of its chief executives were revealed.

> Thousands of fake insurance policies were written up. They were then reinsured with other companies so that Equity funding could generate an immediate cash flow. Fake death certificates for fictitious policyholders were forged. A leading CPA firm okayed the Equity Funding financial reports. ("This World," *Sunday San Francisco Examiner,* June 9, 1974:33)

In their analysis of the Equity fraud Raymond Dirks and Leonard Gross (1974) assert that the case is not the aberration of an otherwise perfect economic system but rather a logical outcome of the morality that obtains on the New York Stock Exchange, in the insurance industry, in the regulatory agencies, and in the accounting profession. Dirks and Gross found that the Security and Exchange Commission approved Equity's financial statements; insurance commissioners in California, Illinois, and other states found no wrongdoing; and over twenty Equity employees, including the board chairman and corporation president, knew of the hoax. The authors concluded that the Equity fraud would not have been possible except for the general atmosphere of "deception" and "opportunism" that pervades the whole insurance industry.

The cases of the Equity Corporation and the Penn Central Railroad are remarkable only in that they were of such magnitude that they received widespread public attention. They are, however, only the tip of an iceberg of industrial espionage, corporate conspiracy, law violation, and open contempt for the public interest. In each of these two cases, as in countless others, legal remedies were nonexistent or rarely enforced. Corporate officials are given special privileges, defended by expensive and prestigious law firms, and treated as noncriminals because of the use of regulatory agencies to administer controls. The privileged use their enormous wealth to win the favor of high government officials to "handle" their cases in a manner that least disrupts normal corporate functioning. The magnitude of corporate crimes are staggering to the average imagination—so much so that the average citizen is at a loss to measure the social harm (personal troubles) that is inflicted upon him by these crimes. How ironic that crimes of such magnitude go unpunished in an age when petty criminals are pursued in the name of law and order. Is this not a demonstration that the crimes of the privileged are permitted because they really represent the underpinnings of the "free enterprise system"? The corporate criminal and his treatment by the legal system is a perfect example of the connections between crime and privilege.

Many criminologists who write about upper-world crime suggest that the solution to this problem is to awaken a sleeping citizenry and have them push for full application of the laws governing corporate activity. This approach restricts the analysis to the level of personal problems of milieu by placing blame upon the "apathetic" citizenry. These writers assume that elected officials respond more or less automatically to citizen complaints. Nothing could be more politically naïve. The reader of the daily newspaper knows that corporations hire professional lobbyists to present the company's side of the story to government officials. The staff and management of federal and state regulatory agencies is dominated by men who formerly held positions in the industry that they now are supposed to regulate. Elected officials receive legal and illegal, personal and political cash contributions from major corporations. Moreover, corporation boards, their legal firms, and corporate managers make up the substantial pool of men who are recruited into high-level government service. The bias toward free enterprise is guaranteed both philosophically and practically. Although there is some evidence that the public outcry that emerged in the wake of certain exposés or consumer crusades has resulted in new legislation, close examination reveals that the final versions of specific new laws are heavily compromised to accommodate business interests. Most of these so-called consumer protection laws have few resources with which officials can investigate and prosecute complaints.

A second error of certain writers on corporate crime is that they make a sharp distinction between acts in violation of existing laws and practices that are not legally regulated. Gilbert Geis, for example, believes that to study activities that are not legally prohibited is to destroy the intellectual tradition of criminology. But he misses the obvious relationship between the upper-world criminal and the forming of laws governing business. Whether or not we decide to label as crimes certain acts that are not now outlawed by the penal codes of the fifty states, the analytic linkage between corporate crime and ordinary business practice is crucial to our understanding of the public issues underlying the phenomenon of upper-world crime.

A useful tool in understanding corporate crime, as well as other crimes by the privileged, is the Marxian construct of the surplus-value theory of labor. A simple example illustrates this concept. Imagine that an industrialist purchases $85 worth of shoe leather and pays workers $10 to convert the materials into finished products. He later sells the shoes for $100 and thereby realizes a $5 profit. Marxists would argue that the difference between the cost of production and the value of the merchandise on the marketplace is derived from the unpaid labor of the workers. Profit, then, is the unpaid-for portion of labor rendered by the workers. Marxists assert that the value of the goods is created totally from the laborers' toils. This unpaid-for labor is conceived of as theft or exploitation. The use of technology or capital merely increases and makes more efficient the level of exploitation of the labor force. The concept of private property merely masks this labor theft by separating the production process from the fact of ownership. In this sense, all industrial enterprise is associated with crime.

The surplus-value theory prompts us to ask about the origins of great wealth in this country. We know that landed aristocrats were generally driven from America during the Revolutionary War. This does not mean that there were not men who owned large portions of land; rather, land ownership in the new republic was not supported by an ideology of aristocracy or privilege through birth rights. The wealth of this nation was produced first by usurping the land of Native Americans, and later through the unpaid-for labor of African peoples brought to this country as slaves.

Historian Eric Williams has demonstrated that the industrial system in England and later in the United States depended heavily upon the slave trade and slave labor. Industries such as shipping, agriculture, and cotton manufacturing—as well as smaller industries, such as those that made the chains to hold slaves—were derivatives of the inhuman system of slavery. Williams cited "an eighteenth century writer [who] estimated that the sterling value of the 303,737 slaves carried in the 878 Liverpool ships between 1783 and 1793 at over fifteen million pounds" (Williams, 1966:36). Williams estimated that the English city of Liverpool alone cleared a net profit of 300,000 pounds per year during the 1780s. The wealth produced by the "human cargoes" was enormous, and many writers agree with Williams that the slave trade produced the financial surplus that supported the English and American industrial revolutions. Later, as the economy moved towards railroad construction, large numbers of Chinese and Irish workers were brought to this country as contract laborers. They were paid little and subjected to long, hard work days. Mexican people were impressed into agricultural labor in the Southwest and West. In the East, European immigrants—especially women and children—worked in sweatshops for minimal wages. Convict labor was sometimes used in competition with wage labor, although not to the extent reported in the early labor movement. Convict labor, as well as the labor of children and women, was used by capitalists to depress the amount of wages paid to men.

Sordid and brutal exploitation of labor produced the capital and wealth that was transformed in the second half of the nineteenth century into the great industrial empires of Morgan, Carnegie, Rockefeller, Astor, and Harriman. During this period the consolidation of capital through industrial violence and fraud merely continued a tradition of savage exploitation of humans and their labor. The Progressive era produced an extreme concentration of wealth in a few hands. Kolko has demonstrated that this inequality of wealth has remained virtually unchanged to the present (Kolko, in Skolnick and Currie, 1970:23–31). The period 1880–1920 was also filled with changes from laissez-faire, robber-baron capitalism to a newer system of corporate capitalism, which focused more upon financial control of industrial enterprises. It should be emphasized that for many years both systems competed side by side for power. Some believe that the imperialist expansion of the United States after the Spanish-American War strengthened the economic power of the finance capitalists, who were able to use their banking resources to exploit overseas labor, natural resources, and markets for American production.

To recapitulate, the accumulation of wealth in the United States, which has always been associated with power, is intimately linked with the genocide of native Americans in order to seize their lands and with the exploitation of labor—slave labor; the labor provided by Chinese and other immigrant workers; and the labor of the men, women, and children of the working class in general. This surplus value was multiplied by the China trade, the centralization of capital by the industrial giants, and the growth of imperialism after the Spanish-American War. Certainly, technology played a role in the escalation of wealth, but the effect of technology may be understood in terms of producing more effective and efficient means of labor theft. Much of the industrial activity during the age of the robber barons (1880–1920) was proscribed by existing laws but was permitted to occur because the control of the rich over the government and the legal system allowed the privileged to be lawless.

In the context of the intimate relationship among crime, wealth, and privilege described above, the criminality of the contemporary upper-world offender appears a logical extension of business morality, which has remained unchanged to the present. Third-world people continue to be exploited the most—as marginal members of the work force, as residents of racial ghettos that produce enormous wealth to slum landlords, and as victims of firms that sell inferior goods at the highest prices and credit institutions that charge the highest possible interest rates. In the urban core we see the continuance of the profitable racial slum that is replaced only when the prerogatives of industrial development dictate that the land slum dwellers inhabit can be used to even greater profit. The crime of the upper world is rooted in the basic relationships of the racial, capitalist society—social privilege and private property. These relationships are the bases of the wealth and power harnessed by the ruling class to maintain a social order designed for self-aggrandizement. One result of this is that "as news of the higher immoralities breaks, [the power elite] often say, 'Well, another one got caught today,' thereby implying that the cases disclosed are not odd events involving occasional characters but symptoms of a widespread condition. There is good probative evidence that they are right." (Mills, 1959b:344)

The State: Partner to Privilege

The interconnection between crime and privilege is most explicit in the structure of the modern liberal state and its relationship to the ruling class. Social theorists from Marx to Weber have defined the state in terms of its monopoly on the means of legitimate violence; that is, the distinctive character of the political state consists of its exercise of violence through its police, military, and prisons. Violence is legitimized through a carefully constructed ideology in support of repression by the state. For example, a criminal is arrested and punished "because he has broken the law," or the government wiretaps the phones of certain citizens to "protect national security."

Revolutionary theorists who have had to confront state repression offer us the most detailed analysis of state functioning. It will be useful to explore their line of reasoning. Lenin's classic statement on the nature of the state is that "the state is an instrument of class domination, an organ of repression of one class by another; its aim is the creation of 'order' which it legalizes and perpetuates this oppression by moderating the collisions between the classes." (Lenin, 1968:9)

In Marxist theory, the state is viewed as something that is external to society and that comes into existence during times of class strife in order to maintain the domination of the more powerful class. An example taken from the research of Richard Cloward and Francis Piven (1971) provides a clear illustration of state emergence. The authors seek to explain the reasons for changes in welfare laws and in the treatment of the poor. The overall argument is that welfare rolls expand or contract according to the need of the state to stave off potential social revolution. In peaceful times the welfare system contracts, but during periods of social disruption it expands. In the course of their historical analysis, Cloward and Piven discuss socioeconomic developments in the French town of Lyons, during the middle of the sixteenth century.

Lyons was a relatively peaceful city for most of the first half of the sixteenth century. The poor were cared for through a private system of charity administered by the Catholic clergy. The consolidation of land holdings into larger estates (known as the European enclosure movement) forced thousands of peasants off their land and into the cities. In the cities, the displaced peasants found little or no employment; they occupied the role of a surplus labor pool. The economic plight of the peasants worsened: public begging, starvation in the streets, and a wave of thefts and burglaries took place. The bourgeois class of the town grew more and more fearful of the criminality and lawlessness of the peasants. Soon there were bread riots and a form of institutionalized riot known as the mob. Armed workers marched through the streets of Lyons and in one skirmish the city was nearly burned to the ground.

In response to a level of class struggle that could not be tolerated, the ruling class of the town decided to develop a coordinated charity-giving system that would control the seemingly dangerous poor. Resources for the charity were commonly pooled. An early step involved a survey of the number of the poor. Definitions were constructed to differentiate between the "worthy" and the "unworthy" poor for the purposes of distributing food and clothing. Finally, poorhouses were constructed and the indigent were confined and put to work there. In this historical example, we see in microcosm the basic elements of the modern welfare system. Some might object that we no longer have poorhouses, but that claim would be shaken if those persons were to visit county jails in America, which house persons arrested for vagrancy, loitering, nonpayment of bills, or nonsupport of family. Exact population figures are difficult to collect, but the vast majority of persons serving sentences in county jails in the United States are confined for the crimes mentioned above, as well as for public drunkenness and gambling.[9] These offense categories, which are generally labeled "offenses against the public order," account for more than half the arrests made by police in any given year, according to F.B.I. statistics.

The Lyons case illustrates how a private, informal system of charity regulated by religious doctrines was transformed, under the threat of class warfare, into a centralized, formalized welfare system backed by the local militia and the poorhouses.[10] The welfare system of Lyons is an example of the growth of a parcel of the state machinery in response to social disruption.

A different example of how the state responds to threats (or perceived threats) upon the privilege structure is seen in the actions of the United States government against the Industrial Workers of the World during the Progressive era. The IWW—or the Wobblies, as IWW members were popularly referred to, was an early forerunner of the American Labor movement. Although the Wobblies had an unfounded reputation for violence, their legend departs from reality. According to Melvyn Dubofsky, a historian of the IWW,

> Wobblies did not carry bombs, nor burn harvest fields, nor destroy timber, nor depend upon the machine that works with a trigger. Instead

[9] The F.B.I. estimated that there were 91,000 arrests for vagrancy in 1971 *(Uniform Crime Reports*, p. 115). The same year, 1.8 million persons were arrested for public drunkenness.

[10] It is fascinating that during this historical period criminals, the poor, homeless children, the physically handicapped, and the mentally ill were all housed together and "treated" in the same manner. Later, these groups would be confined in separate facilities under the rubric of reform. But in the sixteenth-century poorhouse, one sees the concept of a dangerous class that included several types of social deviants and that was seen as a common threat by the ruling class.

> they tried in their own ways to comprehend the nature and dynamics of capitalist society, and through increased knowledge, as well as through revolutionary activism, to develop a better system for the organization and function of the American economy. (Dubofsky, 1969:147)

The Wobblies grew out of an organization known as the Western Federation of Miners. In 1903, the governor of Colorado responded to the pleas of mine owners by dispatching troops to break a strike by arresting the union's leaders. Military officials charged with halting the strike declared, "To hell with the Constitution, we are not going by the Constitution." They appealed to a "military necessity which recognized no laws, either civil or social" (quoted in Wolfe, 1973:26). The pattern of calling federal and later state militia to stop IWW organizing efforts was commonplace throughout the first two decades of the twentieth century.

Initially, industrial leaders organized bands of vigilantes to harass and repress IWW activities. These private armies often operated with the approval of state officials during a period when government leaders could not find legal restraints to apply to IWW activities. Subsequently, in many states, such as Pennsylvania, a state police was organized as a "reform" to replace the private police employed by industrialists in labor struggles. Some state officials wanted a "cleaner" alternative to the vigilante groups as a means of stopping the activities of the IWW.

Perhaps most frustrating for corporate and government officials was their inability to prosecute labor agitators. IWW members did not appear to violate any criminal laws; their major transgressions were that they refused to work, threatened to hold strikes, and maintained an ideology opposed to capitalism. Because it was believed that many of the IWW membership were European immigrants, the Bureau of Immigration under Woodrow Wilson's administration was called in to investigate. After carefully examining IWW writings, the investigators were forced to admit that the writings of the IWW "contain nothing in direct advocacy of anarchism, active opposition to organized government, or the destruction of property, private or public" (quoted in Wolfe, 1973:27).

Lacking the authority of criminal laws to stop the Wobblies, government officials seized upon the device of using deportation hearings under federal naturalization laws. The Supreme Court had defined deportation proceedings as not punitive but administrative hearings, and, thus, due process rights were not considered binding.[11] Many judges in these deportation hearings interpreted IWW membership as evidence of disloyalty or bad character, and many alien members of the Wobblies were immediately deported on these grounds. Court decisions were later formalized into United States policy by act of Congress in the Naturalization Law of 1917.

State actions covered by immigration laws did not solve the problem of how to stop nonaliens engaged in labor organizing. Federal officials continued to use espionage and naturalization laws to investigate IWW records and activities. There was continued pressure from industrial leaders to prosecute the Wobblies. Finally, in Chicago most of the leaders of the IWW were charged with conspiracy.

> Legal trials were urged upon the Wilson administration by lumber interests in the Northwest. They needed a strategy that would break the IWW but at the same time not win it many adherents among skilled lumberjacks, who were difficult to find at that time because of the war. (Wolfe, 1973:28)

The Wobblies were charged with conspiracy to obstruct the carrying out of certain laws, including the Draft Law, and conspiracy against industrial production. The jury deliberated less than an hour and found more than 100 defendants guilty of over 400 criminal charges. The Chicago verdict prompted other jurisdictions to complete criminal proceedings against lesser IWW leaders. Wolfe reports that 83 of the Chicago defendants received prison terms ranging from 5 to 20 years; 12 of the convicted Wobblies served lesser time in local jails or federal prisons; and 5 were released by the court (*Ibid.,* p. 36). Dubofsky observed that the trial of the Wobblies proved to be an effective political strategy.

> The law had clearly proven to be an effective instrument of repression. When vigilantes had deported miners from Bisbee or had lynched (Frank) Little in Butte, the American conscience had been troubled. But when the Justice Department arrested suspected criminals, indicted them before impartial judges and randomly selected petit juries—that is, when the formal requirements of due process were observed—the American conscience rested easier. (Dubofsky, 1969:443)

[11] The cases used by the Supreme Court involved the deportation of Chinese and Japanese immigrants. The cases that established the "nonpunitive" aspects were Fong Yue Ting v. U.S., 149 U.S. 698 (1893); and the Japanese Immigrant Case, 189 U.S. 86 (1903).

The case of the Wobblies is virtually a prototype of government repression against groups that challenge the privilege structure of the United States. The familiar pattern includes violence by non-state agents (e.g., the Klan) conducted by vigilantes with the approval of state agents, uses of legal proceedings such as grand juries or administrative hearings to harass individuals without the guarantees of due process protections, and, finally, the use of criminal charges to attack the activities of political dissidents. The dynamics of state repression seen in the IWW case are also seen in the experiences of Japanese-Americans placed in concentration camps after the outbreak of World War Two, black Americans fighting for civil rights in the South, members of the Vietnam peace movement in America, and members of the Black Panther Party. State violence is "justified" through legal proceedings that attempt to mask the explicitly political goals of stopping threats to the existing privilege structure.

State action during periods of intense social conflict is crucial both as an efficient means of organizing violence against political rebels and as a way to mask the thrust of political oppression by appealing to apparently "neutral or objective" criteria, symbolized by criminal law. Alan Wolfe cited the Italian Marxist, Gramsci, in describing this double-sided character of the state: "Those in power, according to Gramsci, keep themselves there not only forcibly, but also by developing a certain cultural style that makes their rule seem inevitable." (Wolfe, 1973:19) Gramsci used the word *hegemony* to describe this process. The essence of hegemony is captured in Lyndon Johnson's famous remark that the U.S. goal in Southeast Asia was "to win the hearts and minds of the Vietnamese people." Gwyn Williams provides this excellent description of the process.

> . . . an order in which a certain way of life and thought is dominant, in which one concept of reality is diffused throughout the society in all its institutional and private manifestations, informing with its spirit all taste, morality, customs, religious and political principles, and all social relations, particularly in their intellectual and moral connotations. (Williams, 1960:587)

Wolfe tells us that for revolutionary groups the struggle against the hegemonic function of the state is as important as the physical struggle. The culture and ideology of oppression permits the ruling class to justify the use of new forms of power against the "dangerous classes."

Dominant political theory in the United States portrays the state as either a neutral arbiter of disputes between conflicting interest groups (pluralist theory) or as the political expression of a widespread social consensus (democratic or consensus theory). Criminologists have usually adhered to the consensus theory, although some iconoclasts have espoused the pluralist or conflict perspective. Today, conventional criminology seems to be moving towards acceptance of the pluralist viewpoint. Criminal justice administrators describe themselves as "caught" between the two political extremes of "conservatives" and "militants," both of whom advocate different kinds of crime prevention strategies. These administrators seek to present themselves as neutral or above political struggles; they appear to occupy a reasoned, middle-ground stance. Frequently, they appeal to the law and to legal channels to bring about reform, although criminal justice officials are often partisans in legal battles over procedural reform. Police and judicial and correctional personnel maintain powerful and well-financed lobby groups to influence legislative decision making. Within their organizations they retain legal units that challenge court decisions that are inconsistent with their bureaucratic philosophy and routines. Moreover, criminologists and crime control officials offer "expert" testimony before various policy-making bodies.

Despite an increasing acceptance of a model of society composed of "conflicting interest groups" and the alleged "value conflicts" that trouble criminologists and criminal justice administrators, the advocacy of these persons remains remarkably consistent over time with the dominant racial, capitalist social order. The most potent argument, from their perspective, is the ultimate authority of law to resolve all political conflicts. They appear to dismiss the relationship of the privilege structure to the legal system, and in so doing they place the *idea of law* in the center of their contribution to the hegemonic processes of the state. There is probably no more important line of investigation for the New Criminology than the discovery of "dialectics of legal repression." [12]

The Dialectics of Legal Repression

In his study of judicial response to the black ghetto riots of the 1960s Isaac Balbus developed a rather sophisticated theoretical framework that may be used to understand legal repression and various

[12] This phrase was coined by Isaac Balbus in *The Dialectics of Legal Repression* (1973).

criminological issues. Balbus emphasized two dimensions or conflicts of the liberal state: the need for the ruling elite to respond to revolutionary threats and at the same time maximize its legitimacy; and the conflict between formal and substantive principles of justice.

The first of these tensions is created by the need to respond to violence immediately and to bring about its end. But the liberal state cannot act ruthlessly to suppress violence because this runs the risk of destroying the powerful mythology that the state is benign and of increasing the political constituency of the rebels. The state is thus caught "between the immediate interest in ending the violence and the long-range interest in maximizing legitimacy and thereby limiting revolutionary potential" (Balbus, 1973:3). Elites attempt to resolve this conflict between short-run and long-range political expediency by appealing to the rule of law, due process of law, or "formal rationality" to dispose of threats against the social order. The appeal to formal codes of law supports the authority of the state but tends to constrain the elites from using its fullest organization of violence. During periods of intense social struggle, such as labor unrest during the times of the Wobblies or the race riots of the 1960s, the principles of formal legal restraint are relaxed or openly violated because the nature of the threat makes long-run legitimacy a secondary goal to the maintenance of order. Moreover, as Balbus argues, the application of the principles of formal rationality (or individual justice) to the problem of law violation heightens the contradictions of the social structure in terms of substantive rationality (or social justice). To understand this relationship, we must explore the relationship between formal rationality or law and the growth of capitalism.

Balbus noted that both

> Marx and Weber, the two greatest students of capitalist development, stressed the inseparable links between the origins of capitalism and the growth of political equality, and hence the crucial significance of equality before the law as a legitimating principle of the liberal state. (*Ibid.,* p.4)

The development of a universal legal institution, under which all were equal, was a critical weapon for the rising bourgeoisie, who wished to eliminate the arbitrariness and importance of aristocratic privilege that limited their profit-making activities. Weber in particular saw the connection between an economic system that valued rational calculation, and fixed legal principles that permitted the emerging capitalist class to predict the legal consequences of its action.

> To those who had interests in the commodity market, the rationalization and systematization of the law in general and . . . the increasing calculability of the functioning of the legal process in particular, constituted one of the important conditions of the existence of economic enterprise intended to function with stability, and especially, of capitalistic enterprise, which cannot do without legal security. (Weber, in Balbus, 1973:4)

A highly rationalized and predictable economic organization required a legal system that could insulate its activities from the shifting control of any particular set of political actors. Formal legal rationality was at its base a set of substantive and procedural norms to be applied both to the government and the governed. In this context the judicial aspect of the state evolved into formally autonomous units, distinct from the legislature or the executive. "The 'separation of powers' characteristic of the liberal state is thus properly understood as one of the political-legal expressions of the requisites of a capitalist economic order." (Balbus, 1973:5)

Marx focused his attack upon formal rationality in terms of political emancipation. He viewed civil liberties, due process, and voting rights as expressions of the interests of the bourgeois class.

> None of the supposed rights of man, therefore, go beyond the egoistic man, man as he is, as a member of civil society; that is, an individual separated from the community, withdrawn into himself, preoccupied with his private interest and acting in accordance with his private caprice. (Marx, in Bottomore, 1963:26)

Marx believed that *political emancipation* was based upon self-interest and competition. In contrast, *human emancipation* meant the realization of the fullest collective human potential; and this would occur only in a socialist social order.

Balbus concluded that the combination of formal legal equality and extreme economic inequality is the hallmark of the liberal state: "If the law is indifferent to this distinction between the rich and the poor, it follows that the law will necessarily support and maintain this distinction" (Balbus, 1973:5). The poor and those who are denied the benefits of privilege are not served by the "equal" system of justice. Their demands that the law administer the equalization of economic and social privilege is blocked by judges and administrators who proclaim that the requirements of formal, rational law prohibit special favors. A direct example of this conflict can be seen in the dispute in the early 1970s over Affirmative Action programs in employment and education. Liberals are horrified by such attacks upon the principle of "equal opportunity" and they betray the economic base of their position by asserting that Affirmative Action would *destroy the system of merit* so necessary for a highly technical industrial economy. The quest for substantive or social justice is subordinated to the maintenance of formal legal equality.

Bertrand Russell observed that the concept of human liberty has been profaned by men of power who have violated the principle and invoked it in self-interest. Historian Sidney Willhelm believes that the principle of equality before the law has ominous implications for black Americans.

> The shift from preindustrial production in Southern agriculture and from industrial to automatic technology throughout the nation furnishes an opportunity for White America to create a new racial strategy in keeping with its anti-Negro tradition. With the departure of the Negro as a contributor to the production of goods and services, White America perceives the chance to comply with Negro demands for equality. The nation moves more and more towards equality with new dedication as the Negro is less conspicuous in the nation's economy. There is greater willingness to grant the Negro's demand to be placed on par with whites simply because this is one of the most effective means of dispensing with the Negro. (Willhelm, 1971:229)

Willhelm believes that the subordination of the black American in the economic order to continual unemployment and underemployment will lead to the self-destruction of the race. Feelings of frustration and the demeaning social status of being permanently jobless create conditions of inward despair and powerlessness. In the face of this structural oppression, legal equality and equality of opportunity are cruel lies promoted by the privileged to buttress the American Dream.

The core of the hegemonic function of formal rationality is to leave open the possibility that those without privilege may obtain it by conforming to cultural patterns and rules laid down by the ruling class. The exploited labor force, who provide the foundation for the political-economic order, are presented with the twin principles of their "legal right" to rise up in the social structure and their "right" to express grievances through a "politically neutral" state machinery of courts and administrative agencies. Balbus suggests that "the existence of formal legal rationality and the concepts of due process, an autonomous judicial sphere, and civil liberties which it entails are the essential props of the capitalist order" (Balbus, 1973:6).

The contradiction inherent in the pursuit of legal equality in the liberal state is that it brings into sharp focus persistent socioeconomic inequalities. The goal of formal rationality is betrayed by the existence of class distinctions. This has been epitomized by the emphasis of some liberal critiques of the criminal justice system upon the larger goal of social justice. In *Struggle for Justice* the American Friends Service Committee concluded that

> to the extent . . . that equal justice is correlated with equality of status, influence, and economic power, the construction of a just system of criminal justice in an unjust society is a contradiction in terms. (AFSC, 1971:16)

Wolfgang and Cohen found that

> equal justice requires the appointment of many more qualified judges from minority-group ranks, as well as the recruitment of minority-group lawyers, probation officers and others in the administration of justice. Our juries must be made representative of the entire population and the taint of prejudice must be eradicated from the judicial process. (Wolfgang and Cohen, 1970:109)

These liberal critics of criminal justice locate the problem in the maldistribution of power, status, and wealth in the society. Thus, "to give content to the normal principle of equality before the law, it may ultimately be necessary to abolish the very economic system that spawns that principle" (Balbus, 1973:6).

Few liberal criminologists take their analysis to its logical conclusion—an attack upon the privilege system that enforces social injustice. In place of advocating substantive justice, the adherents of liberal ideology reemphasize their faith in legal procedures. Attention is thus directed towards preventing gross violations of legal principles by the state while everyday forms of oppression continue unchallenged. Political elites are generally willing to confine their activities within the limits of formal legality, but in times of crisis they move swiftly on the path of political expediency. The Watergate scandal is instructive in this context. The offense of the Nixon administration in the eyes of men such as Sam Ervin, Lowell Weicker, and Barry Goldwater was not the general level of oppression it exerted over the underclasses but that its activities were performed outside of formal legal criteria. The clamor over the abuse of power was confined to criticism of actions that violated the ruling-class standard of formal rationality. In most other matters of ideology, the President and most of his critics were in agreement. By breaking the rules of the game the Watergate offenders exposed the reality that the game is fixed on behalf of those who support and enforce the system of privilege.

"Repression by formal rationality implies that every effort will be made to employ ordinary legal procedures and the ordinary sanctioning mechanisms in the course of the elite effort to repress collective violence." (*Ibid.,* p.12) For the elite the first benefit of this form of repression is that it affect the consciousness of participants in revolutionary activities. The attempt to place the label of "crime" on participants' behavior is intended to convince them that their behavior signifies nothing more than an outbreak of massive criminality. The legal system "confronts individual events as something permanently established and exactly defined" (Lukacs, 1971:97). The efforts to fit the actions of those who participated in the urban race riots into "ordinary" legal categories is intended to define the behavior in terms of activities that are usually disapproved of. To fit the events under the rubric of "crime" in effect robs them of their political implications. This in turn works against the growth of mass solidarity and consciousness, an important issue for the rioters.

Once the "criminalization" process is under way, the public debate is deflected away from the demands or grievances of the protestors; instead, it focuses upon the severity of the punishment that they should receive. This process reduces the likelihood that the participants in a political struggle will gain adherents from other oppressed groups or from sympathetic members of the elite: "To confer the status 'criminal' on the participants is to strongly suggest the illegitimacy and even the potential criminality of expressions of support for the participants." (Balbus, 1973:12) The sympathetic elite will be unwilling to attack the principles of formal rationality and will thus focus their efforts upon guaranteeing a fair and impartial judicial hearing for the defendants. But in this narrow concern for the rights of the accused, the sympathizers implicitly accept the state definition of the activity of the accused.

The dynamic of legal repression is not limited to the containment of violencc or to the suppression of radicals, such as the Wobblies. Formal legal rationality depoliticizes the functioning of the criminal justice system. Legal doctrines assert that the only relevant question to ask is whether the proscribed behavior was actually committed by the accused. Apart from mental incompetency or gross mental illness, the question of substantive motivation for the act is deemed irrelevant to the determination of guilt. In theory, neither the "why" nor the "who" of the act is important. The rules of criminal procedure replace the explicit conflict between the offender and the state with a fact-finding conflict contested by two equal combatants. The ideal type of criminal justice prevents the issues of ideology, class, or race from entering the meaning of "crime" or "criminal." According to the pure model of formal rationality, any injustices that result from the system must be caused by improper criteria applied during "discretionary" aspects of the process (such as the decision to arrest, the decision to prosecute, or the fixing of a sentence). Once the defendant is found guilty, he or she no longer is "protected" by the rigid limits of formal rationality but rather is almost totally under the power of penal authorities. This is particularly well illustrated by the fact that prisoners and parolees have virtually no legal rights.

By underscoring the workings of legal repression in the ordinary criminal case, I am not substituting a romantic notion that all criminals act out of political motivation or consider themselves rebels. Rather, I am arguing that the total impact of legal formalism is to remove the political significance from the operation of the criminal justice system. Moreover, the empirical reality of the legal process is a massive processing of criminal defendants through guilty pleas, the result of which is a virtual assembly-line form of justice. In most jurisdictions, 80 to 90 percent of criminal defendants plead guilty and thus forfeit the basic protections of due process. Jerome Skolnick described this system as follows:

> Under these circumstances of mass administration of criminal justice, presumptions necessarily run to regularity and administrative efficiency. The negation of the presumption of innocence permeates the entire system of justice . . . all involved in the system, the defense attorneys and judges, as well as the prosecutors and policemen, operate according to a working presumption of the guilt of those accused of crime. That the accused is entitled to counsel is an accepted part of the system, but this guarantee implies no specific affirmation of 'adversaryness' in an interactional sense. (Skolnick, 1966:241)

Even this practice of "bargain justice" is shrouded in the rituals of formal rationality. The accused who has entered a guilty plea on the promise of judicial leniency is asked by the judge in open court if his plea is made freely without coercion or promise. The defendant is expected to reply that no one has made him any promises. If he tells the truth about the process of threats and promises, the entire legal fiction is exposed.

The ideology of formal justice is intended to affect the consciousness of the everyday criminal defendant in the same way that it affects the consciousness of the urban rioters described by Balbus. Political or social significance is removed from the transaction. The label "criminal" discredits the accused's claims of social injustice and lessens the possibility that others in his or her environment or in the larger community will feel compassion for his or her plight. The relationship between the offender's actions and the larger system of economic and political oppression is denied by the ideology of law. Through its denial of the culpability of the privileged in the social reality of the criminal event, the state masks its own crimes and supports the appearance of the moral superiority of the privileged classes. David Matza, referring to the liberal state by the name Leviathan, observes that

> in its avid concern for public order and safety, implemented through police force and penal policy, Leviathan is vindicated. By pursuing evil and producing the *appearance* of good, the state reveals its abiding method—the perpetuation of its good name in the face of its own propensities for violence, conquest and destruction. Guarded by a collective representation in which theft and violence reside in a dangerous class, morally elevated by its correctional quest, the state achieves the legitimacy of pacific intention and the acceptance of legality—even when it goes to war and massively perpetrates activities it has allegedly banned from the world. But that, the reader may say, is a different matter altogether. So says Leviathan—and that is the final point of the collective representation. (Matza, 1969:197)

In this final passage of his book, *Becoming Deviant,* Matza describes the role of the state in its pursuit of the criminal as a powerful support for the hegemonic domination by the privileged class.

Crime and the Maintenance of Privilege

Our discussion of formal legal rationality as a technique for supporting the rule of privilege by depoliticizing challenges against state authority can be extended to consider the more general role of crime in solidifying the power of the privilege structure. In particular, we need to explore the relationship between crime and cultural domination by ruling groups.

Culture may be defined as a system of guidelines for behavior—a code of "Thou shalls" and "Thou shall nots." Rules defined by culture are reinforced by the rewarding of those who conform and the censuring of those who break the rules. The authority of one group to dictate the boundaries of culture is supported by appeals to the presumed special qualities of the ruling group, which set them above the rest of the population. Cultural domination may be anchored in appeals to tradition, in claims of the superiority of the ruling clique, or, as seen above, in appeals to abstract legal systems that are portrayed as neutral or objective. Although the ultimate base of cultural control is the power of an elite to use violence to enforce its belief system, the elite attempts to ensure the long life of its structure of privilege by convincing the mass of the population of the "correctness" of a particular set of moral demands.

The units of society that promote and enforce cultural demands the most are the institutions of that society—the family, the economy, the military, religious orders, educational institutions, and political institutions. Cultural domination is accomplished when the viewpoints of one particular group control and direct each of these social institutions. This control is achieved through the definition of the components or *roles* within each institution, through the definition of the goals of each institution of the social structure, and through control of the behavior that will occur within each institution. Complete control, or hegemony, is achieved when the boundaries or contours of acceptable behavior are so ingrained in mass thinking that they are taken for granted.

Consider, for example, the educational institution. Roles or positions are defined in terms of the flow of decision making and the responsibility of maintaining the order of the institution. Roles such as administrator, school-board member, teacher, and student are defined in terms of norms that limit who may play a particular role, how participants in each of the roles should behave towards those in the other roles, and what common goals members should pursue. All of these norms of accepted behavior are consistent with the larger structure of privilege, which is the central organizing principle of the entire social structure. For example, teachers are supposed to hold certain "credentials" indicating that they have successfully completed performance in other roles, such as student or apprentice teacher. Racial and sexual characteristics of teachers may be determined by law (in rigid caste systems), by customs or rituals, or by a screening process established by prior institutions. In a liberal democratic social structure, distinctions of birth, race, and sex are rarely made explicit; rather, they are maintained through the screening procedures practiced by those in power. In the case of teachers, tests, examinations, and recruiting and hiring practices maintain the distinctions defined by privilege. Recently, third-world educators in a number of jurisdictions have challenged the criteria of employment used by licensing authorities, such as state boards of education, that limit the numbers of third world teachers, even those who hold the necessary degree and professional requirements. The privilege structure may exert subtler but equally powerful controls over the occupation of particular roles by carefully defining the appropriate aspirations of persons in particular fields. In our society, female teachers learn through their institutional participation to aspire to teach only at the elementary or high school level. College teaching is culturally defined as primarily a male profession. Similarly, third-world teachers often expect to be assigned to racially segregated or inferior schools. Individuals who try to violate the norms regulating role occupancy are ridiculed, discouraged, or confronted with special constraints.

Norms governing proper behavior for those in particular roles constitute the next step in the domination process. Teachers are expected to maintain a specific form of authority inside the classroom. Their interactions with students are sharply limited. The choice of curriculum, texts, and teaching aids is tolerated only within certain bounds. This toleration, limited though it is, enhances the mythology that the teacher has freedom over his or her actions. In most cases control need not be all that rigid, but in certain special areas (in particular, where the institutional order is threatened) the control is complete. Thus, the teacher may select educational material from an *approved* list and may present *acceptable* ideas in a variety of formats, but unapproved books or unapproved ideas may result in censure or dismissal. Conformity is conspicuously rewarded and deviance is discouraged by means of a wide assortment of techniques.

The specific and overall objectives of the educational process are usually taken from the larger structure of privilege. Some observers suggest that the primary function of schools is to prepare the student to accept authority in other institutions. Students are not so much educated as they are taught to accept the cultural direction of superiors. Success in the educational process is measured in relation to the individuals compliance with the established order. Schools channel students into educational tracks that direct them into specific places in the economic structure. Questioning of alternatives is often discouraged or punished. For example, the black child who rejects the images of the white, middle-class, suburban ideal projected by textbooks may be defined as a "slow learner" or a "troublemaker." The tactic is to define the rebellion in terms of an individual problem that can be handled by some form of counseling or punishment. School officials attempt to explain the student's problem in a manner that isolates the "content" of the complaint from the violation of school rules. Parents and other adults are enlisted to support the establishment position in the dispute. Most insidiously, the student who rebels is confronted with powerful but apparently benevolent "helpers" who try to convince the student that the difficulty is a personal inadequacy that can be cured with effort and self-discipline. Unless the individual has strong self-confidence or the support of others, the conflict may be translated into feelings of guilt and failure. Even the person who "drops out" or refuses to conform may be plagued with continuing self-doubts and apprehensions. These doubts are confirmed because the institutions of society act as gatekeepers to the culturally defined benefits of privilege, such as jobs, income, social recognition, and educational attainments. Self-doubts are further exploited through the use of intelligence tests, aptitude tests, and psychological instruments, which appear to be objective but are actually biased in terms of values and cultural traits that are consistent with the maintenance of privilege.

Criminologist Albert Cohen described part of this process in his study, *Delinquent Boys* (1955). Cohen argued that in a society characterized by a class structure, the values and norms of one class will be used to measure the achievement of those from the lower classes.[13] Members of the lower class cannot measure up to these standards and, according to Cohen, must form some defense mechanism to explain away feelings of failure. Individuals who are cut off from group supports

[13] Cohen and a number of other theorists described the dominant value system as "middle-class." Cohen's mistake was to confuse the role of the middle class—enforcing norms of behavior—with the role of the upper class—establishing the behavior norms for each class. Correct behavior is not simply imitation of the ruling class; rather, it consists of the moral demands appropriate for each subgrouping of society that supports the privilege of the ruling class. For example, the idea that the middle and lower classes must defer gratification is a means of guaranteeing that the under classes do not challenge the existing distribution of goods and services. Members of the ruling class are more often "conspicuous consumers" who place little value upon deferred gratification for themselves. The postponement of rewards for others is an integral part of the ideology that continues the labor exploitation of others by the privileged class.

may define their feelings as personal inadequacies, but if like-situated persons are allowed to share their troubles, they will form a collective response, which Cohen calls "the delinquent subculture." The delinquents reject the dominant value system, turning it "upside down" by behavior that violates its content. Cohen believes that "effective interaction" among the socially rejected is the crucial variable in the formation of the delinquent group's negative response.

Although several authors have questioned whether the delinquent response is indeed a total repudiation of the dominant culture, Cohen's insight into the process of forming a rebellious response is quite important. One may view Cohen's theory as a classic insight into colonial domination, in which the oppressor must pay careful and continuous attention to the psychological response of the oppressed. Successful colonial regimes attempt to control all social arenas in which "effective interaction" among the downtrodden may take place—schools, churches, and other gathering places that may breed revolutionary movements. The subjugated are prevented from congregating in situations that are beyond the scrutiny of the political regime. Police and army units patrol the streets; secret meetings are invaded and the participants arrested; and the ability of the oppressed to organize is rigidly limited by colonial law. Moreover, the teachers and clergy, the social workers and psychiatrists of the ruling class are introduced into the communities of the oppressed to direct and monitor the content of their interaction in schools, churches, recreation facilities, and street corners. By limiting opportunities for the oppressed to discuss the forces involved in their domination, the colonial regime complements its armed control.

From the perspective of the privileged, crimes are those actions that directly threaten their *physical and cultural* hegemony. It is crucial that the ruling class attempt to convince the mass of the population that criminal acts are a threat to every member of the social order. And although it is true that many criminal acts cause tremendous suffering among the oppressed, the social rituals of law enforcement and the administration of justice are designed to support the dominance of the privileged as a first priority and to protect individuals as a second-order priority except when policies of nonenforcement might directly threaten the established order.

This process can be readily observed in the enforcement of laws against crimes such as murder, theft, robbery, and rape. Statistics gathered from police agencies as well as from victim surveys have shown that poor people and third-world people make up a disproportionate number of the victims of "serious crime" with the exception of thefts of large amounts of property. Public discussion of serious crime, however, tends to distort and overemphasize the threat of victimization to all segments of the society. This often results in elaborate preparations by the well off to protect themselves, including the purchase of guns and the installation of expensive alarm systems.

The lower classes are less likely to report crimes to the police because they are skeptical that the police will do anything about their victimization. Whereas the privileged have insurance protection against theft, which requires that the individual report the theft to the authorities, those who cannot obtain insurance or afford to pay high premiums perceive that their economic losses will increase if they report a crime to the police. If the authorities apprehend a suspect, the victim must often miss several days at work to assist law enforcement officers and testify in court. Few property crimes (less than 20 percent according to national figures) result in somebody being taken into custody. Even if a conviction is obtained, it is rare that the victim has his or her property returned. *The end of a successful prosecution means that the state and its legal code is upheld.* The victim can derive only the most indirect satisfaction from the knowledge that some person is placed on probation or sent to prison. The person who steps forward to aid the state in its prosecution can rarely expect any protection if the offender chooses to retaliate. Frequently, treatment by legal authorities of poor and third-world victims is abusive and degrading.[14] This process was illustrated in Chapter One in the discussion of rape.

A similar contradiction occurs in the case of violent crimes. The state's actions against the violent offender have little or no benefits for the victim. The loss of life, the trauma of violent crime, the medical costs, and the fears of future attacks are all borne by the victim, who is likely to be third-world and poor. The vindication and glory of conviction belongs to the state and its agents. In this light one can see that the state offers almost no protection to victims or future victims of criminal acts. Rather, by publicly espousing its role as public protector, the state seeks to make the citizenry dependent upon its agents for their security. The state seeks to exert a monopoly over crime control and crime prevention efforts. This position is supported by claims of the professional expertise of criminal justice personnel in crime abatement activities.

One of the most pervasive myths promoted on behalf of the state's

[14] Report of the National Advisory Commission on Civil Disorders (1968).

monopoly on crime control is that the natural tendency of citizens would be to act as uncontrolled vigilante groups. In the past year, newspapers have carried accounts of "mobs" of citizens apprehending and beating criminal offenders. The image of the courageous western lawman protecting his prisoner from the angry lynch mob is one of our most popular cultural images. But as we saw in the case of the Wobblies, law enforcement personnel offered covert encouragement to citizen vigilantes, and in the many tragic lynchings in the American South, legal officials looked the other way or participated in mob actions in unofficial capacities. The isolated acts of mob crime control in the modern urban setting can be understood as an expression of the despair of the powerless that the police will not respond to their cries for help, not as evidence of a basic human predisposition to mob justice. Underenforcement of the law has been a consistent complaint of the under classes. They perceive the police as unresponsive to their security and often corrupt in law enforcement practices. A history of neglected crimes within the ghettos of poor and third-world people has fostered a deep-seated distrust and hostility of law enforcement personnel by those at the bottom of the social structure.

Police and court actions in pursuing justice among the oppressed reinforce the inferior position of the under classes. One learns that the values of life and personal safety in the communities of the oppressed are not as crucial as protecting the privileged. Examples of the dual system of justice are daily reminders of the gradations of privilege. Following a number of killings in San Francisco's Chinatown, a public official assured the tourist trade that no Caucasians had been involved in the murders. A Philadelphia police officer remarked that he didn't care if gang kids (predominantly black) killed themselves, as long as innocent victims were not harmed. Studies by Wolfgang and Riedel (1973) and Bullock (1961), among others, have documented that the most severe sentences are given to black offenders who victimize whites.

> Since the victims of most of all the Negroes committed for . . . (murder) were also Negroes, local norms tolerate a less rigorous enforcement of the law. (In the case of property crimes) When the Negro is the offender, his attack is usually against the property of a white person. Local norms are less tolerant, for the motivation to protect white property and to protect "white" society against disorder is stronger than the motivation to protect "Negro" society. (Bullock, in Wolfgang and Cohen, 1970:82)

The dual system of justice is an integral part of the race privilege system. The differential response to white and black victimization supports the idea that white life is more valuable than black life. In addition, lax law enforcement perpetuates the mythology that black people are prone to criminality. Police encourage law breaking by their attitude of noninvolvement. In certain areas of criminality, such as gambling, drug sales, or prostitution, police may act on behalf of organized criminal interests.[15]

It has been argued that the pattern of ignoring the internal criminality of black communities changed after the urban riots of the 1960s. The evidence is not conclusive, but it appears that proportionately more police resources have been placed in black communities. This, in turn, has contributed to the arrest of a larger number of blacks. Despite the increase in sworn personnel patrolling black communities and despite a larger volume of arrests, one still hears continued complaints by communities that the police will not respond to calls about crimes in progress. Community residents argue that the police continue to use a "containment strategy"—vigorous law enforcement of offenders who commit offenses in the central business districts and in white communities but a disregard for crimes in black residential areas. Law enforcement activity in the ghetto is designed to curtail threats to the white privilege structure.

Another way of looking at benefits to the privilege system from crime control activities is to examine the symbolic significance of the official crime control posture. The manipulation of the symbolic interpretation of social events is central to the cultural preservation of privilege. Certain behaviors may be identical in physical details—such as the taking of life in war, the killing of a fleeing felon, or the shooting of a friend in a personal dispute—but the official definition of these actions will almost always conform to the cultural prerequisites of the privileged class. The culture supplies justifications, or "vocabularies of motives" in C. Wright Mills's terminology. Such vocabularies comprise motives that excuse the behavior of the actor in one situation and condemn him or her in another. The policeman is "justified" in shooting the felon *because he is enforcing the law;* the soldier is excused *because of higher orders* or the supposed necessities of war; but the criminal is seen as "irrational"—that is, operating outside the realm of acceptable vocabularies of motives. Even if the motives of the offender

[15] See the findings of the Knapp Commission and the Pennsylvania Crime Commission on police corruption in New York and Philadelphia, respectively.

are known, they are considered illegitimate and outside the bounds of the culturally imposed rules of social interaction.

Likewise, in the case of theft there exist rationales that explain the theft of the natural resources of third-world countries or the financial exploitation of the poor, but the taking of property in a criminal event is portrayed as qualitatively different. Fraudulent business practices might be justified in terms of the vocabulary of motives of the competitive marketplace, or imperialist exploitation may be defended in terms of the need for industrial growth and development; thus, the offender is placed "beyond incrimination" (Kennedy, 1970). The petty offender who steals to keep from starving or who burglarizes houses to obtain money to survive in the status system at the bottom of the social structure is not excused because condoning his actions would be to admit to the generality of theft and exploitation in the entire society. Laws that protect the sanctity of private property primarily benefit those who have the most property. Laws that condemn individual violence are primarily designed to support the monopoly on violence that is claimed by the state.

Crime functions to further enhance the hegemony of the privileged through the creation of a criminal stereotype. This involves an attempt to distinguish between the lawbreaker and the law-abiding citizen. The lawbreaker will be imbued with all of the negative traits contained in the culture. The purpose of the construction of this criminal stereotype is to convince law-abiding citizens that they are superior to the offender. Dennis Chapman (1968) has observed that the most typical image of the criminal is that of the convicted offender who is in prison. When we think of the criminal, the picture of the confined convict comes immediately to mind. This is important in light of several studies that appear to show that most adults in our society have committed serious crimes. Often, these studies use confidential questionnaires that determine the criminal behavior of subjects from all segments of the social structure. A study by Wallerstein and Wyle (1947) found that 91 percent of adult male subjects admitted to having committed at least one felony. In a series of self-report studies Williams and Gold (1972) found that criminality appears to be broadly distributed throughout the social order; this finding contrasts with official police statistics, which make crime appear to be contained primarily in the lower class. These data seem to suggest that laws, particularly those involving protection of property, are not deeply internalized by the mass of the population.[16]

[16] Lack of respect for private property can be observed in the looting activities of residents of

The stereotype of the *captured* criminal takes on great importance for the powerful, who wish to protect their wealth from the actions of the masses. The harsh social contempt heaped upon the criminal serves as an object lesson to other members of the society to live by the rules laid down by those in power.

The stereotype of the "irrationality" or personal inadequacy of the criminal denies that the offender may be responding both rationally and strategically to the life-chances offered by the racist, capitalist social order. Our images of the criminal deny that the goals and motivation of everyday life, such as competition, social recognition, personal greed, and interpersonal aggression, are the same as the "crude and base" motives that cause criminals to act as they do. If one breaks through the hegemonic myths about the criminal, however, one discovers that many law violators refer to a vocabulary of motivation taken directly from the ideology of the privileged.[17] For example, gang youths often refer to the heroic portrayals of violence in films and on television in their discussions of gang fighting: "It's just like cowboys and Indians." Ghetto hustlers inform us that "it's survival of the fittest"—a key element in the social theory of Herbert Spencer, who was honored and feted by the British and American capitalist class of the late nineteenth century. Many of those involved in crime believe that the "straights" have a "superior hustle" that allows them to make money without large risks of capture and punishment. Our previous discussion of upper-world crime strongly supports their view. A few criminologists, following Taft (1942), have maintained that the primary causes of crime may be such aspects of the American value structure as the glorification of violence, the encouragement of competition, the emphasis upon material possessions, and the support of "rugged individual" aggression. Critics of this approach attempt to argue that crime can be found in virtually every society, but they ignore the issue of amount of criminality, and they ignore the special nature of the rationales used to explain crime in capitalist societies that exhibit sharp class and racial stratification.

The punishment and handling of the criminal is set in an elaborate social ritual that reinforces the cultural dominance of the ruling class. Criminal trials take place in often elegantly appointed courtrooms

areas struck by natural disasters. Such natural catastrophes appear to release the cultural constraint of "Thou shall not steal" in most members of the social structure.

[17] If we understand how the oppressed internalize some of the myths of the privileged, then it is not difficult for us to understand crimes in which both the offender and the victim are members of the under class.

before a judge who is cloaked in the religious garb of the black robe. Religious and national paraphernalia are used as props in support of the moral quality of the criminal prosecution. Moreover, the current mode of demonology, be it religious, scientific, or political, is used to explain the reasons behind the criminal's actions. The supposed benevolence of the state is symbolized by the use of social work and psychiatric treatment to effect the offender's reintegration into the "morally blameless" mainstream of society. The reality of correctional practice is, however, strikingly at odds with the images of benevolence projected by the court and the correctional system.

Criminality is used as a cultural device to mask the inequities of the social structure. During periods of intense political struggle, the powerful will attempt to convince the population that the gravest danger is the decline of "law and order."

> Thus, if the "crime problem" is perceived as *the* urgent issue, other issues are relegated to a position of secondary importance in the structuring of our social priorities. In this sense the problem of crime becomes an ideological one in that it serves to conceal or distort the underlying reality of the social damage inflicted by such problems as permanent inflation, chronic unemployment, the ever-widening gap between those earning high and low incomes, class conflict, a seemingly perpetual housing shortage, and environmental damage. These issues are given a marginal sense of importance. (Blumberg, 1974:4)

Blumberg notes that federal expenditures for law enforcement services have constituted one of the largest growth areas of the federal budget. Since 1971 the combined expenditures of all levels of government for criminal justice are $10.1 billion, nearly triple the amount spent on crime control a decade ago. This greater investment in crime control was made in response to the perceived threats to social stability that occurred during the last half of the 1960s. During these years, ghetto revolts, antiwar protests, the student movement, and community organization efforts were all seen by the elite and their agents as symptomatic of a decline of law and order. In this historical period as well as others, the myth of crime waves served to mask adjustments in the social control network that were required to maintain the dominance of privilege. For example, legislation in the 1930s restricting immigration to the United States by certain "undesirable races" was justified because of the presumed criminality of those groups. During the 1950s educators debated whether lower-class youngsters should be channeled into special nonacademic programs in order to reduce juvenile delinquency in schools. Recently, Congress considered the testimony of a well-known criminologist who asserted that eliminating the minimum wage law for persons under eighteen would reduce street violence. In each of these cases the issue of crime was imposed to cover the actual dimensions of racial, class, or political conflict.

According to sociologist Kai Erickson, crime waves appear at those points in time when the elite requires a moral redefinition of the boundaries of cultural domination. Such moral redefinitions take place when an elite group is threatened by the under classes or when competition occurs between competing segments of the elite. Erickson asserts that crime rates are largely a function of the capacity of the crime control mechanisms to detect, apprehend, and prosecute offenders. He argues that the rate of crime will remain fairly constant unless the powerful use more energy and resources in the pursuit of criminals. His book *The Wayward Puritans* (1966) details three "crime waves" that occurred in colonial New England, each during a time of intense doctrinal and political conflict among the leaders of the colonists. These periods of intense pursuit of criminals relocate moral boundaries and solidified identification with the dominant cultural group and its belief system.

> . . . certain kinds of religious ritual, dance ceremony, and other traditional pageantry can dramatize the difference between "we" and "they" by portraying a symbolic encounter between the two. But on the whole members of a community inform one another about the placement of their boundaries by participating in the confrontations which occur when persons who venture out to the edges of the group are met by policing agents whose special business is to guard the cultural integrity of the community. Whether these confrontations take the form of criminal trials, excommunication hearings, courts-martial, or even psychiatric case conferences, they act as boundary-maintenance devices in that they demonstrate to whatever audience is concerned where the line is drawn between behavior that belongs to the special universe of the group and behavior that does not. (Erickson, 1966:11)

Erickson's description of the cultural-reinforcing function of the treatment of deviants is quite useful, except that he fails to distinguish between preindustrial societies without rigid stratification systems and postindustrial societies that are structured according to race and class differences. He relies upon the ideas of Emile Durkheim, who developed the notion of a "collective conscience" in his review of descriptions of preliterate societies contained in the literature of nineteenth-century anthropology. Both Durkheim and Erickson define culture as something that emerges from group consensus and tradition. Neither of them employs a conception of culture that is imposed upon the population by a particular group. This oversight is particularly ironic in Erickson's study because his case studies concern elite realignments to maintain cultural hegemony. Of course, Puritan Massachusetts did not contain the elaborate class and status distinctions of postindustrial American society, but Erickson might have achieved a better understanding of the relationship between crime and privilege had he considered the treatment of blacks and native Americans by the Puritan colonists. Despite this weakness, Erickson's study provides an excellent illustration of the attempt by the privileged to consolidate power through "moral crusades" against deviants.[18]

The Progressive era (1880–1920), which witnessed the rise of the modern criminal justice system, was characterized by intense conflict between the ruling class and the under class and between the older white, Protestant elite that was locally based and the newly and nationally powerful robber barons and corporate capitalists. The white, Protestant upper class defended their position of laissez-faire economics, social Darwinism, and the preservation of racial purity. They were suspicious of government, which they believed was dominated by the robber barons and the big-city political bosses. This group was preoccupied with fears that aliens and inferior racial stocks would take over their Anglo-Saxon America.

The competing elite group was no less white and Protestant (although a few wealthy Jews and Catholics were permitted at the periphery of the inner circle), but they tended to favor policies that promised greater profits. Thus, they supported continued immigration, which expanded the surplus labor pool. They favored the growth of state institutions that would protect their economic interests; the National Guard, for instance, could be used to break up labor strikes. They favored the introduction of scientific or rational means of maintaining social order. Their ideology towards social problems such as crime was a form of reformed social Darwinism rather than the direct Darwinism of the white Protestant elite.

[18] See Joseph Gusfield's study of the Prohibition movement (1963), in which he argues that the temperance movement was a "symbolic crusade" of the WASP establishment against urban immigrants and the "evils" of the city. Platt's *The Child Savers* (1969) provides further illustration of this point.

During this period of elite conflict and social disruption, criminologists and penologists developed ideas about crime that resonated with the interests of both elite groups, but they ultimately sided with the political and economic interests of the corporate capitalists. Boostrom (1974) describes the four key elements of this criminological ideology as follows:

> 1. The establishment of the idea that crime is an alien phenomenon in American society. Crime was claimed to be a phenomenon principally associated with alien, non-white, non-Protestant groups. Crime was also seen as associated with the growth of urban-industrial centers stimulated by technological progress.
>
> 2. A second key was the effort by the correctional reformers to disassociate their ideas and panaceas from those of radical groups such as socialists.
>
> 3. The third key issue was the effort to differentiate progressive correctional reform ideas from the perspective of social Darwinism. Correctional reformers lobbied for creative government intervention (the positive state) to solve social problems while conservative social Darwinists argued for the limitation of government to reactive police powers.
>
> 4. The fourth key issue was the establishment of the idea that the solution to the crime problem in modern society would require social support for special "scientific" expertise and intervention. Social psychological theories emphasizing the need for the development of the corporate personality and the social control of the rebellious individual were developed by the new academic social science. (Boostrom, 1974:2–3)

This description of the ideology of academic criminology and correctional reform reveals the uses to which the stereotype of the criminal can be put in order to solidify control of the ruling class and to perpetuate its concepts of social organization. The new discipline of criminology began to develop programs designed to "tame" not only the criminal but also those at the bottom of the social hierarchy, particularly those who challenged the stability of the social order. Today, the criminal stereotype and mythology about crime help build ideological walls that imprison us in the contradictions of our social life.

The Dimensions of Power and Privilege

To complete our discussion of the relationship between crime and privilege, we need to examine in some detail the gradations of power and privilege. Throughout our analysis we have used terms such as "elites," "ruling classes," "the powerful," and the "privileged." In this section we attempt to clarify the relations among some of these terms as they relate to the different levels of power. This discussion necessarily takes us into the area of political theory. Such an excursion is exceedingly rare in the conventional criminological literature. Most standard texts in criminology adopt the view that power is distributed according to the rules established by the Constitution and other laws. Leadership, for this group, is an expression of the popular will or majority. In short, the problem of power is resolved by definitions. Another group of criminologists see the nation being ruled by a series of minorities, each competing for a share of power. They view political decision making as a process of conflict followed by compromise. Each of the conflicting parties is supposed to get some of what it wants, but no group consistently dominates the centers of power. This perspective, known as "pluralist theory," dominates American political science. A smaller group of criminologists have acknowledged the unequal distribution of power in the society but this group leaves the categories of the "powerful" or the "elite" as unexamined aspects of the social structure.

Perhaps the most abiding contribution of C. Wright Mills to political sociology was his description of the concentration of power in the hands of a small "power elite." Mills noted that although interest groups could be located throughout the society, these groups varied in their power and level of organization. Mills argued that the development of large-scale bureaucracies inhibited the equal expression of interests because it concentrated power in a few positions within the bureaucratic network. The occupants of powerful positions are further organized into "rings of influence," which Mills described as aspects of the military, political, and industrial establishments.

Mills's perspective of the power elite has been attacked by theorists who are more influenced by Marxist political economics, such as Sweezy (in Domhoff and Ballard, 1968:115–32) and Milliband (1969).[19] To these theorists the locus of power resides with those who command the economic institutions rather than the formal political offices. The center of power is a ruling class, which is defined by its control over the institutions of industrial production. The ruling class perspective is further elaborated into differing amounts of power within various sectors of the economy. Competing theories by analysts

[19] Mills's political theory depends extensively upon the political sociology of Max Weber.

of political power leave us confused and unclear about the real locus of power in our society.

The major constraint upon developing theoretical precision in this area is the near impossibility of penetrating the centers of power and thereby studying empirically the exercise of power. Most often, we are faced with the after-the-fact reality of decision making; in such instances we must attempt to construct retrospectively the dynamics of the power process. The workings of power are often cloaked in official rhetoric that stresses the complexity and multisided nature of political decision making in specific policy areas.

Wolfe suggests that there is a way out of this theoretical quagmire that will yield helpful insights into the operation of power and privilege. His first suggestion is that there is no reason to accept either side of the debate between the advocates of a power elite and the theorists of a ruling class: "Power in America exists at both the economic and political levels. The point is not to subsume arbitrarily one under the other but to recognize the different kinds of power associated with each and to examine the conditions under which one is more important than the other." (Wolfe, 1973:61–62) Both concepts are useful in interpreting the dimensions of power in America. Wolfe suggests that power is a relational concept—that is, one exerts power in relation to something else. One group may hold power over a second group, which, in turn, exerts power over a third entity. The middle group exerts power in certain instances but is controlled in others. In discussions of the workings of criminal justice the middle levels of power constitute an important group to study. Wolfe presents a model of power that is structured both horizontally and vertically. The vertical dimension includes upper, middle, and lower levels of power; at the lower level, persons possess little or no influence on societal decision making. Horizontally, Wolfe considers both the economic and political components of power. For Wolfe, the capitalist social structure continually evolves in order to accommodate changes in the nature of capitalism itself; thus, the economically powerful shape society in its most basic aspects. Within the framework of the capitalist economic order, political leaders and political institutions decide on and implement policy matters. Political decision making is crucial, but "the range of available policy options are all perceived to be within the basic structure of a capitalist society. In this sense, the economic positions have primary importance to which the political positions are secondary." (*Ibid.*, p. 62)

Wolfe has provided a valuable paradigm of the upper, middle, and lower levels of power; these levels are distinguished according to policy formulation and policy implementation (*Ibid.*, p. 63). Of direct interest to students of criminology are the middle levels of power, which contain the political decision makers and the administrators of the criminal justice system. But, the character of local law enforcement as well as the lawmaking powers of state officials sometimes blind us to the interconnections between national and state decision making. The study of crime and privilege demands that we explore the role that linkages between national and local bases of power play in the formulation and implementation of criminal justice policies. Let us first describe some features of the highest circles of influence before moving onto a discussion of middle-level power.

Wolfe argues that the highest levels of power demonstrate his distinction between shaping policy and deciding upon policy. The theorists of pluralism tend to focus upon the immediate events and prominent personalities which precede policy decisions and are thus hypnotized by the complex infighting that occurs in governmental institutions. The pluralists assume that capitalism is inevitable and that it is taken for granted, and this leads them to ignore the persons and institutions that strengthen and support the capitalist economic system. But as Wolfe observes,

> American capitalism did not mysteriously appear. It was brought into being by some very powerful people. It is continuously reproduced by others who spend most of their time trying to ensure its reproduction. In order, then, to speak of the ruling class, we would be mistaken to look at political decision making but must focus instead on those whose activities define the parameters of the system and reproduce those parameters on a day to day basis. (*Ibid.*, p. 64)

The ruling class consists of those individuals who create and perpetuate the consensus about values and goals that shapes political, economic, and social thinking. This consensus consists of the political values that are considered the only legitimate ones. The most important ideas at present include the following:

1. Representative democracy under the Constitution is the best form of government.
2. Private-enterprise capitalism is the only legitimate economic system; the state has a role in solving problems posed by that system.
3. America is the best nation on the face of the earth and it is essential to

defend the country against foreign enemies. This value most often takes the form of suspicions and animosity toward nations and individuals that practice some form of Communism.

It is important to remember that this consensus is brought into being by those with substantial power and that the content of the consensus changes over time. Prior to the 1950s and 1960s protection of the civil rights of black Americans was not part of the official American rhetoric. Before the Progressive era, state intervention in the workings of the free-market economy was considered unthinkable. Similarly, attitudes towards the Soviet Union and China have undergone substantial revisions by the ruling class.

Wolfe believes that the ideology and structure of the current ruling class originated with the struggles over power that occurred during the Progressive era: "The commitment to modern corporate liberalism came into being in the years 1900–1920, when a group of men associated with the National Civic Federation rejected both Social Darwinism on the Right and Socialism on the Left, combining elements of both into a new ideology that has essentially governed America since that time." (*Ibid.*, p. 65) [20] Today the ruling class plays the central role in maintaining that ideology.

The ruling class consists of a subset of the wealthiest and most privileged persons in our society. For Wolfe, this class consists of the most "politicized members of the upper class" (*Ibid.*, p. 66). Sociologist E. Digby Baltzell developed a measure of the ruling class by identifying individuals who were listed in the *Social Register* (an index of Americans with high social status) and *Who's Who* (a guide to persons who are prominent in terms of position, accomplishments, and wealth). The prototypical member of the ruling class is from a rich and/or aristocratic family; might head a major corporation or serve on the board of directors of several major corporations; or might hold a high government position. Ruling class members might also be presidents of major foundations or partners in prestigious law firms. Although some of them hold elected office, members of the ruling class are more likely to be advisors or counselors to a person in the executive branch of government. Halberstam notes that the ruling class seeks to exert power but avoid public scrutiny. Members of the ruling elite who are constantly in the public eye are often distrusted by fellow members (Halberstam, 1972, pp. 11–14).

[20] In his massive history of the American role in Vietnam, David Halberstam (1972) argues that American foreign policy has been controlled by the same ideology and the same ruling clique since the first two decades of the twentieth century.

Wolfe suggests that one of the major vehicles for the ruling class are *transmission belts*—institutions that do not make policy but seek to shape policy alternatives. The Council on Foreign Relations, which publishes the influential journal *Foreign Policy*, is a major transmission belt in the international field. The domestic equivalent to this council is the Committee for Economic Development (CED), which seeks to promote an international philosophy among capitalists. The CED portrays itself as nonpartisan and nonpolitical, and its stated objective is to "promote stable economic growth with rising living standards and increasing opportunities for all and to strengthen the concepts and institutions essential to progress in a free society" (quoted in Quinney, 1974:83). CED is organized to actively promote the capitalist economic and social order. In 1972 CED published "Reducing Crime and Assuring Justice" (1972), a policy document written by a panel of corporate directors and one university official.

The CED's report on crime proposes solutions cast in the framework of modern business practice—namely to modernize and make more efficient the current operations of the criminal justice system. The report singles out the administrative and organizational inefficiency of law enforcement and court operations and proposes a total overhaul of the criminal justice system, including "a redistribution of responsibilities, functions and financial support among various levels of government" (quoted in Quinney, 1974:84). Local governments would remain in charge of urban policing, but all other criminal justice functions would be drawn together under "a strong, centralized Department of Justice" (*Ibid.*). The new federal authority would coordinate the attack upon crime as well as provide financial incentives to local government to reorganize state and local operations. The CED report avoids questions about the role of the social structure in crime; rather, it defines the solution to the crime issue in terms of more efficient administration. The report suggests that "the national government has no constitutional or direct authority for law enforcement," but "when customary patterns of federalism break down in the face of critical and widespread problems, the people of this country have on many occasions turned to the national government" (*Ibid.*, p. 85). The CED report suggests that the national crisis of crime demands immediate action, and it advocates the building of support for its ideas by *opinion leaders* and the majority of the citizenry.

This "unofficial" report of the CED is consistent with determinations by national advisory panels or presidential crime commissions. Quinney (1974:51–94) provides excellent documentation showing that virtually all national commissions are dominated by members of the ruling class. Moreover, the study and advisory functions of national commissions are enhanced by the activities of other crucial transmission belts, such as the Ford Foundation, the Russell Sage Foundation, and the Rockefeller Foundation, which fund demonstration projects and various other experimental reforms with the intent of stimulating government action. In all of these activities the consensus of the ruling class is elaborated and publicized.

One of the most significant traits of the ruling class is the intricate network of relationships among its members. Corporations, foundations, private organizations, and social clubs contain overlapping memberships drawn from this ruling clique.[21] Members of the ruling class dominate the boards of regents or trustees of virtually every major American university and, in turn, hire educational administrators who are sympathetic to the ideals of corporate capitalism and who will make sure that "radical" ideas are not permitted to flourish on university campuses. University administration is guided nowadays by the principles of the modern corporation, complete with computerized decision making, production quotas, and budget allocation processes, all of which are keyed to the techno-economic needs of the business community. In addition to universities and foundations, the ruling class controls most of the mass media, which is a primary instrument for molding the consciousness of the mass of the citizenry. The everyday reader of the newspapers receives his primary information about crime and criminal justice through that medium. Moreover, the portrayal of police and court functioning on television is usually consistent with the ideology of the ruling class concerning crime control. Although it is beyond the scope of this book, the analysis of the content of media reports on crime and crime control would be an important area for investigation by the New Criminology.

As we have indicated earlier, the ruling class is most potent in the role of "public servant." In this role they define themselves as capable of transcending the special interests of particular groups and claim to operate in the "national interest." But the empirical examination of the functioning of ruling-class members reveals that the "national" or "public" interest is actually the interest of the capitalist class.

Our discussion of the influence of the ruling elite is not meant to minimize the influence of those who hold positions of great political power. The political power structure is composed partly of members of

[21] See Baltzell (1964), Domhoff (1967), and Kolko (1969).

the ruling class and partly of persons who are sympathetic to the interests of that class. The relationship between the two groups is often cemented by the generous campaign contributions and media support that the ruling class extends to the politically ambitious. The ruling class does not have to dominate the political structure because this might threaten the hegemonic mythology that the society is open and democratic (the prime example of which is the notion that any child may grow up to be president of the United States). This need to buttress the American Myth means that a slight chance exists that someone could be elected who is opposed to the influence of the ruling class, but the full weight of the transmission belts is generally marshaled to prevent this from occurring. One of our most pervasive political myths suggests that political leaders who gain power primarily through mass support may become dictators. When "populist" politicians gain national attention there is usually an attempt to discredit them, or, failing this, steps are taken to integrate them into the regular party structure through limited compromises. The ruling class exercises a limited amount of toleration and compromises in order to sustain its overall hegemonic ascendancy.

Intimately related to the upper levels of power are the middle levels, which in the economic sphere are composed of corporate managers and in the political realm, officials of state and local government. The primary function of the middle level of power is to carry out the policy imperatives of the most powerful. The economic and political managers exert a great deal of influence over the lives of ordinary citizens but are ultimately responsible to those above them. The middle power structure can be observed most directly in the functioning of state and local government. The strategic location of economic and political managers at the local level gives them direct authority over crime control. Penal codes are passed by state legislatures, operating standards for law enforcement agencies are established by executive branches of state government, and financial support for day-to-day operations comes from state and local budgets. Police chiefs, for example, are extremely sensitive to the wishes of local business associations such as chambers of commerce, and they frequently speak before civic associations such as the Lions Club, the Rotary Club, and the Junior Chamber of Commerce. These groups are generally composed of managers of large corporations in specific localities and owners of medium-sized businesses.

At the middle levels of power certain nonbusiness groups, such as labor unions, farm bureaus, or moderate organizations representing ethnic groups, play some role in policy formulation in criminal justice areas. Although these groups, as well as some professional associations (notably state bar associations), have influence in criminal justice affairs, this influence exists within the boundaries of the ideology and power defined by national elites.

Sometimes one can observe battles between the locals and the nationals over specific policy matters that might require minor readjustments in power configurations. A good example of this occurred during the massive allocation of criminal justice funding under the auspices of the Law Enforcement Assistance Administration of the U.S. Department of Justice. The original organization of LEAA under the Johnson administration envisioned direct grants from the federal government to localities for the purpose of experimental changes in law enforcement practice. Congressional debate and infighting forced a compromise that would channel monies into state government agencies for local distribution. In virtually every locality vigorous battles were waged over the distribution formulas, often pitting municipal officials against state officials. Throughout the administration of the massive funding program ($1.75 billion alone for the fiscal year 1973) the various sectors of middle-level power fought over the allocation of funding. One of the results of the program was the growth of a powerful political lobby by police agencies, who used their connections at the local level to grab most of the early funds (see Goulden, 1970). Many at the federal level felt that the money was being squandered on purchases of unnecessary equipment or was being used to replace regular agency budgeting. The last few years have seen repeated attempts by the national political structure to guide and direct the allocation of resources. This has been accomplished by imposing rigid funding guidelines, establishing required orders of spending priorities, and disseminating "exemplary projects." For example, the LEAA has generated "prescriptive packages," which describe the approved procedures for setting up programs that are viewed favorably by national officials. In addition, various "think tanks" of the national ruling class, such as the Rand Corporation, the Brookings Institute, and the Mitre Corporation, have received substantial grants to assist localities in improving their criminal justice programs. Most recently, the LEAA established a panel to create National Priorities on Goals and Standards. This national commission—which, like most others, consists of members of the ruling class—defined the new boundaries for policy formulation. And although there is likely to be continued struggle among the middle and upper levels of power over specific issues, the ultimate outcome will probably be some compromise that substantially favors the interests of the national ruling elite.

Normal operations of crime control agencies are constantly being evaluated and studied by national organizations. Such transmission belts as the International Association of Chiefs of Police (and its funding conduit, the Police Foundation), the National Council on Crime and Delinquency, and the American Law Institute are often engaged in drafting "model legislation" or "model codes of standards," which are marketed to state legislatures or other local decision-making bodies.

The ruling-class orientation of the National Council on Crime and Delinquency (NCCD) is an interesting example of the workings of a transmission belt. The NCCD began as an organization of probation and parole officers who wished to upgrade their profession. Helped by a grant from the Ford Foundation, the organization launched a citizen action program comprising 690 members in 21 states. In a study entitled "The Crime Fighters" (1971) Wildeman showed that this supposed representative citizen's group was made up primarily of members of the economic and political ruling elite. He found that 81 percent of the crime fighters occupied top positions of authority in industry, trade, and finance or were professional persons or educators. The remaining 19 percent of the organization was dominated by high-level criminal justice administrators. The composition of this group illustrates how the ruling class, in collaboration with some members of the middle levels of power, form institutions designed to affect the criminal justice system. Such organizations conduct extensive public opinion campaigns to convince the general public of the value and inevitability of their ideas. A most interesting ploy used by this and similar groups is to portray themselves as innovators or reformers who are struggling with the ignorant and stubborn administrators of the law and justice agencies. They likewise portray the general public as ignorant, repressive in orientation toward criminals and in need of their expertise to understand the crime problem.

Directly serving agencies and larger transmission belts are professionals, who form with agency administrators the lowest stratum of the middle level of power. Lawyers, social scientists, and psychologists and/or psychiatrists and social workers play a crucial role in maintaining the mythology that crime control activities are politically neutral, based upon scientific principles, and basically benevolent. Professionals are chiefly responsible for producing "new knowledge" about improved methods of crime control and for educating many criminal justice workers. University-trained crime experts help develop and rationalize state crime policies while masking their ideological commitment through claims of scientific or professional neutrality. It is important in this context to recall that the sociological definition of a professional is one who renders a service that *cannot be properly evaluated by clients*; thus, the ethics and practice of the professionals are regulated through self-policing by professional associations. The overriding bias of the professional class is to maintain distance between themselves and the public or their clients. This insulation of professional practice from public accountability is one of the major advantages of the professional class in its crime control dealings. As we indicated in the first chapter, the theoretical and practical orientations of the professionals are almost always circumscribed by the policy frameworks of the ruling elite and the upper reaches of the middle levels of power.

There is a substantial question as to where to place criminal justice workers in this paradigm of influence and power. This issue can be resolved only in relation to specific practice objectives. Workers such as policemen, probation and parole officers, assistant district attorneys, public defenders, and correctional personnel may be seen as both *victimizers* and *victims*. They are victimizers in the sense that they directly administer the system's inequitable and unjust practices. Moreover, they may be blamed for numerous instances of brutality, insensitivity, and repressiveness. But this group might also be reviewed as victims in the sense that they perform the "dirty work" that supports the entire structure of privilege. Criminal justice workers are often caught between public condemnation, client contempt, and unreasonable working conditions imposed upon them by superiors. They are also victims of the ideology that they must accept in performing the social dirty work for the upper classes. Low-echelon workers often try to enhance their job status by making claims to professional status or by seeking additional education, which increases their social mobility. Workers' claims to professional status are constantly undermined, however, by stringent work quotas placed upon them, legal guidelines that severely limit their individual options, and the use by agency heads of principles of scientific management that reduce their interactions with others to measurable and computerized inputs and outputs. For example, the extensive use by police agencies of motorized patrol, in which mechanized computer and communications systems are involved, suggests that police officers are little more than chess pieces to be moved around for tactical advantage. The growing union movement among police and correctional officers may be seen as a partial reaction to the exploitation of their labor by agency heads, but this unionization movement (still prohibited by law in most jurisdictions) has generally focused upon bread-and-butter issues or has been manipulated to support right-wing and often racist sociopolitical interests.

There is a lively debate among New Criminologists about the tactics and theory that are appropriate in working with members of the civil servant class. Although their tactics may differ, they agree that this group is a serious political force to be reckoned with. The last decade has witnessed an enormous growth in the number of persons employed by the criminal justice system. Takagi (1974) estimated that the ranks of police personnel have swelled by 70 percent nationwide in the last ten years. Blumberg (1974) estimates that over *800,000 persons are employed by the crime control enterprise.* These figures and the growing organization among criminal justice workers points out the clear fact that this group cannot be subverted, side-stepped by legislation, or instantly converted to a new occupational orientation. We have few studies describing the work life and frustrations of this group, and neither are there any clear plans to open dialogue among workers, clients of the criminal justice system, and adherents of the New Criminology. We need to explore this area in great detail in order to refine and test out the model of this occupational class as both victims and victimizers.

Our discussion of the dimensions of power and privilege does not pretend to be an adequate description of this enormously complex matter. Because of the newness of the perspective of crime and privilege and the limited amount of empirical research conducted by New Criminologists, we do not as yet have a complete theory that charts the many interrelations and intermediate conflict areas in the network of power and privilege. We hope that as the New Criminology matures we will obtain more than a cursory analysis of the dimensions of power and privilege. Some conventional criminologists have attacked the New Criminology for "having a simplified notion of social stratification." This criticism is partially valid, but conventional criminology does not even attempt to incorporate a discussion of the workings of power and privilege into theories of crime and crime control. To inquire into the dimensions of privilege and its manifestation in various levels of power would endanger the ideological stance of the conventional work on crime and criminal justice. For the most part, conventional criminologists have ignored the implications of crime and privilege, or they have accepted the assumptions and ideology of the corporate liberalism that supports the legitimacy and continued rule of the privileged.

THREE

The Struggle Inside: Prison Writings and the New Criminology

People who come out of prison can build up the country.
Misfortune is a test of people's fidelity.
Those who protest at injustice are people of true merit.
When the prison-doors are opened, the real dragon will fly out.

Ho Chi Minh, *Prison Diary*

More than any other force, the writings and organizing efforts of men and women confined in the nation's prisons have given life and strength to the New Criminology. From behind prison walls have come some of the most articulate and poignant statements about the nature of our social structure and the relationship of crime and privilege. The above quoted poem by Ho Chi Minh, leader of the Vietnamese struggle for national liberation, was the favorite passage of George Jackson, who has become a hero to many oppressed people in this country. Jackson spent most of his young adult life in California prisons—and most of that time in the maximum security units known as "adjustment centers." He was branded a dangerous, violent criminal by prison officials, who ultimately took his life during an alleged escape attempt from San Quentin on August 21, 1971. Supporters of Jackson—and there were many of them world-wide—believed that his murder was the desperate act of a prison system that had confined him for eleven years but could not break his spirit. George Jackson received a hero's funeral in Oakland, California; he was mourned by over 4,000 men, women, and children, whose lives had been profoundly touched by his strength and his courage.

> George Jackson was a complex man, a committed revolutionary, an insightful theoretician, an organizer supreme. Yet, above all the complexities, George was a Black man whose simple love of all living things transcended the chains and the bars, reached beyond the moment in a hungry grasp for the future ideal: the liberation of all mankind.
>
> Such a man can never die . . . George Jackson lives.
>
> (*The Black Panther*, August 18, 1973:3)

Jackson may be located within a long tradition of freedom fighters who have spent long portions of their lives behind bars. It is a staggering but revealing thought that many prominent leaders in the struggle for social justice have been in prison, are in prison now, or are currently facing charges that would result in imprisonment. In this chapter we have selected portions of the prison writings of persons who have substantially advanced our thinking on the subject of crime and privilege. Each writer provides excellent information and analyses that extend and enrich the theoretical perspective on crime and crime control that we have been presented so far. The selections constitute a small slice of a growing and powerful literature of prison writings. One needs only to become a regular reader of newsletters and magazines published by prisoners' groups to become convinced of the depth of feeling and insight among the inmates of our country's jails and prisons.

Some might argue that the prisoners whose writing has received national attention are "political prisoners" and are therefore not representative of the mass of men and women behind bars. To answer this charge, we need to examine the concept of "political prisoner" and understand its wider meaning. In her essay, "The Social Functions of Prisons in the United States" (1971), Bettina Aptheker delineates four types of political prisoners. The first group consists of those "who are prisoners because of their political views and activities or are specially victimized on the basis of class, racial and national oppression" (Aptheker, 1971:58). These individuals, among whom we might include Angela Davis, Huey Newton, Bobby Seale, and Ericka Huggins, have received attention from the guardians of privilege because of their political views and their effective community organizing efforts. The charges brought against them are often the result of the activities of police *agent provocateurs* and undercover "informers." After long, costly trials the charges are generally found to be unsupported, or juries cannot reach verdicts. In several of these trials the state has spent millions of dollars to bring about convictions.

This money, taken directly from criminal justice funding, could have been used for activities that might truly protect the public from serious acts of crime.

The second category of political prisoners are those who, as a result of their political activities, are found guilty of technical violations of law. Such violations might include possession of weapons (for self-defense purposes), violations of Selective Service laws, conspiracy, and violations of local codes, such as "illegal assemblies," trespassing, and marching without a permit. Political prisoners of this type include Martin Luther King, Jr., the Berrigan brothers, and Cesar Chavez. Actions by law enforcement officials are justified in terms of preserving public order or "preventing violence," but it seems clear that arrests are politically motivated and are designed to prevent the open expression of dissent.

A third group of political prisoners have committed a variety of offenses but, lacking adequate representation or political redress, are imprisoned for long terms under inhumane conditions. Literally thousands of persons are in prison because they lack the resources that permit privileged criminals to escape prosecution and punishment. Many from this third group were not originally political in their orientation but became so because of the conditions of their confinement, as well as the organizing efforts of others inside the walls. Most of the leaders of prisoners' unions have come from this class of convicts. Members of this class have participated in prison rebellions, and some have forfeited their lives in struggles to redress prison oppression.

The fourth group of political prisoners are similar to the last group in that they have been convicted of various offenses and may not have had a political outlook when they entered prison. But, this final group has developed a consciousness of the relationship between the conditions of their confinement and the larger social injustices outside the walls.

> As soon as they give expression to their political views they become victims of politically inspired actions against them by the prison administration and the parole boards. They too may become victims of politically inspired frame-ups within the prison. There are many today who were either never guilty of any crime at all, or were guilty of some offense and later developed a political consciousness. (*Ibid.*, pp. 58–59)

This last group includes George Jackson, Eldridge Cleaver, the Soledad Brothers, and Ruchell Magee.

No doubt, a substantial proportion of the inmates in our prisons are not as politically sophisticated as these individuals. Many prisoners cynically reject the unjust social order, but, like most of us on the outside, they do not have a clear idea of an alternative social structure that might be more liberating. They are victims—as much so as the vast majority of Americans—of the oppressive ideology of the privileged. They understand some of the contradictions within the social structure but cling to a belief that through individual effort they will achieve an individual release from oppression that will permit them to only survive. This belief has its parallel on the outside.

> In the ghettoes the white man has built for us, he has forced us not to aspire to greater things, but to view everyday life as *survival*—and in that kind of community, survival is what is respected. (Malcolm X, 1966:90)

The deprivations and daily indignities of the prison environment reinforce the personal despair that leads many prisoners to aspire only to survival. Despite the extreme constraints upon interaction and organization inside the walls, a growing number of inmates are becoming politicized through the efforts of other prisoners. They are learning to interpret their personal troubles in terms of public issues, and they are learning to link their suffering in prison to the conditions of racial, sexual, and class injustice on the outside. In the face of continuing repressiveness within prison by prison administrations, the prisoners' movement continues to grow and flourish. The statements we reprint here increasingly reflect the bolder political consciousness of our nation's prisoners. The category of political prisoner is beginning to merge with the broader category of all prisoners of the racist, capitalist social order.

The first selection we present is an essay by Angela Davis, whose political trial attracted world-wide attention. Ms. Davis is an acknowledged leader of black liberation struggles in the United States. She is now free after being incarcerated for nearly two years for allegedly conspiring with the Soledad defendants in the Marin County shoot-out, in which Jonathan Jackson and a judge were killed. Her co-defendant Ruchell Magee continues to fight prosecution for the events at the Marin County Courthouse. In her essay Ms. Davis briefly recounts the history of the struggles of black people against racial oppression. She discusses the cases of several political prisoners who resisted state oppression. One of her key points is that the state attempts to reduce the significance of political resistance by labeling it as a series of ordinary criminal events. Ms. Davis explains how political prisoners attempt to organize the inmate population by focusing upon the conditions inside prisons and jails. Prisons, to her, are places where the open expression of fascism can be seen. She fears that fascism is a real threat in America and that it can be met only by widespread political organization.

The second selection is the collective appeal of the Panther 21 to Judge Murtagh. This remarkable document on the history of racism and the American legal system was written by thirteen of the defendants in a criminal trial in which twenty-one members of the New York Black Panther Party were tried for conspiracy to bomb police stations, railroads, and department stores and to murder policemen. The thirteen defendants were the only members of the New York Black Panther Party who could be arrested by the police. Their letter to Judge Murtagh is a response to his unprecedented action of recessing the pretrial hearings *indefinitely* until the counsel for the defendants promised that the Panther 21 would show proper respect for the court. Murtagh announced, "This court is responsible for the administration of criminal justice and preventing any reflection upon the image of American justice. That responsibility will be discharged." (Quoted in Lefcourt, 1971:188)

However, the Panther 21 defendants want us to do precisely what Judge Murtagh fears—to reflect upon the image and the reality of American justice. They present a carefully documented account of the legal oppression of black Americans and other people of color in America since 1663. They explain how the purpose of the court and the trial is to maintain the "image" of justice in the face of obvious social injustice. They describe in some detail the dual system of justice for whites and for people of color. They assert that their behavior in the courtroom was incited *not by the actions of their lawyer but by American history.* Their letter to the judge ends with a list of specific rights that were denied them because of the political nature of their prosecution.

Eldridge Cleaver is one of the best-known prison writers. His *Soul On Ice* has been celebrated by some as a literary and sociological classic. Cleaver was active in prison organizing, first with the Muslims and later on behalf of other prison groups. After his release from prison Cleaver became a leader of the Black Panther Party and ran for political office on the ticket of the Peace and Freedom Party. Later, he left the United States in political exile. Though he remains a controversial figure within the black liberation movement, his writings are still considered an important source of political insight. We have reprinted his essay, "Domestic Law and International Order." In this essay Cleaver theorizes that the police and the armed forces are two aspects of the violence potential of the power structure. At the domestic and international levels, respectively, the police and the military protect the way of life of those in power. Cleaver believes that the brutal police actions during the Watts riots demonstrated to American blacks the linkages between their repression and the bloodshed in Vietnam. The agents of repression, according to Cleaver, are "carrying out orders" and are following the plans and policy of the higher-ups. The soldier or the policeman is trained to do his "job" the best way that he can, and he is immersed in the rhetoric and rituals of the American Mythology. Cleaver tells us that the problem is not "trigger-happy cops" but a "trigger-happy social order." He foresees a growing activism among blacks in America who have been asked to die in Vietnam and who return home only to see their families and neighbors dying or being killed in American cities. Perhaps his most important point is that domestic crime control policies directly serve international imperialist "police actions." Domestic crime and international popular resistance are interrelated threats to the privilege structure of the United States. No academic criminologist before Cleaver was able to articulate this vital theoretical relationship.

The last selection is a letter by George Jackson to his attorney Fay Stender, who had accompanied California State Senator Mervyn Dymally on a tour in which they studied racism in California correctional facilities. As a contribution to criminological theory, it is impressive and powerful. Jackson, who always showed an intuitive grasp of the sociological imagination, warns that the inquiry should not become bogged down in "localized conditions" (issues of milieu) but, rather, should focus on socio-political circumstances that breed racism in prisons. He describes how racism is practiced in the details of the prisoner's everyday life. He then describes the horrors and indignities of the "adjustment Centers," which are almost completely filled with black and chicano inmates. Jackson tells of the growing political awareness and militancy of prisoners but foresees that this will result in many deaths. Perhaps seeing the inevitable future, including his own tragic murder and the slaughter of over forty inmates and guards at New York's Attica State Prison, George Jackson wrote, "Men who read Lenin, Fanon, and Che don't riot, 'they mass,' 'they rage,' they dig graves" (Jackson, 1970:31).

The prison writings we have selected are intended to show the theoretical and practical base of current struggles inside prisons. As insights into this current prison movement, these writings contribute substantially to the field of criminology. But in our quest for a truly liberating New Criminology, these writers offer us much more than just this. They open up new channels of investigation, they chart new theories from which to organize action, and, perhaps more importantly, they show how the quest for a New Criminology depends upon the struggle for social justice.

Traditional anthologies in criminology sometimes contain writings by criminals and prisoners. These writings tend to be chosen carefully and are restricted to the works of individuals who have not perceived the linkages between personal troubles and public issues. The narrow perspectives and interpretations of such writings support the ideological positions of the liberal criminologists. Criminals and their writings are data for the criminologist's theoretical models. At best, traditional anthologies of convict writings inform us that some prisoners can think and even articulate their thoughts. This view is blatantly paternalistic, implying that most offenders are incapable of such reasoning and reflection. Quite the opposite is true. For every prison writer who comes to public attention, there are hundreds, perhaps thousands, who feel the same oppression and develop the political consciousness that permits them to spiritually transcend their immediate confinement.

The prison movement does not begin and end with prominent prisoners who become political personalities; the movement is nurtured and sustained by many prisoners who overcome institutional restrictions and stay informed about struggles throughout the prison system and throughout the world. They resist where resistance has the gravest consequences; they speak out where free speech is prohibited. They exhibit hope and courage in places designed to strip the individual of dignity, places designed to foster despair. In this sense, the struggle inside the walls is the backbone of the New Criminology and the movement for social change.

POLITICAL PRISONERS, PRISONS AND BLACK LIBERATION

ANGELA Y. DAVIS

Despite a long history of exalted appeals to man's inherent right of resistance, there has seldom been agreement on how to relate *in practice* to unjust, immoral laws and the oppressive social order from which they emanate. The conservative, who does not dispute the validity of revolutions deeply buried in history, invokes visions of impending anarchy in order to legitimize his demand for absolute obedience. Law and order, with the major emphasis on order, is his watchword. The liberal articulates his sensitiveness to certain of society's intolerable details, but will almost never prescribe methods of resistance which exceed the limits of legality—redress through electoral channels is the liberal's panacea.

In the heart of our pursuit for fundamental human rights, Black people have been continually cautioned to be patient. We are advised that as long as we remain faithful to the *existing* democratic order, the glorious moment will eventually arrive when we will come into our own as full-fledged human beings.

But having been taught by bitter experience, we know that there is a glaring incongruity between democracy and the capitalist economy which is the source of our ills. Regardless of all rhetoric to the contrary, the people are not the ultimate matrix of the laws and the system which governs them—certainly not Black people and other nationally oppressed people, but not even the mass of whites. The people do not exercise decisive control over the determining factors of their lives.

Official assertions that meaningful dissent is always welcome, provided it falls within the boundaries of legality, are frequently a smokescreen obscuring the invitation to acquiesce in oppression. Slavery may have been unrighteous, the constitutional provision for the enslavement of Blacks may have been unjust, but conditions were not to be considered so unbearable (especially since they were

From *If They Come In The Morning*, pp. 27–43, edited by Angela Y. Davis.

profitable to a small circle) as to justify escape and other acts proscribed by law. This was the import of the fugitive slave laws.

Needless to say, the history of the United States has been marred from its inception by an enormous quantity of unjust laws, far too many expressly bolstering the oppression of Black people. Particularized reflections of existing social inequities, these laws have repeatedly borne witness to the exploitative and racist core of the society itself. For Blacks, Chicanos, for all nationally oppressed people, the problem of opposing unjust laws and the social conditions which nourish their growth, has always had immediate practical implications. Our very survival has frequently been a direct function of our skill in forging effective channels of resistance. In resisting, we have sometimes been compelled to openly violate those laws which directly or indirectly buttress our oppression. But even when containing our resistance within the orbit of legality, we have been labeled criminals and have been methodically persecuted by a racist legal apparatus.

Under the ruthless conditions of slavery, the Underground Railroad provided the framework for extra-legal anti-slavery activity pursued by vast numbers of people, both Black and white. Its functioning was in flagrant violation of the fugitive slave laws; those who were apprehended were subjected to severe penalties. Of the innumerable recorded attempts to rescue fugitive slaves from the clutches of slave-catchers, one of the most striking is the case of Anthony Burns, a slave from Virginia, captured in Boston in 1853. A team of his supporters, in attempting to rescue him by force during the course of his trial, engaged the police in a fierce courtroom battle. During the gun fight a prominent abolitionist, Thomas Wentworth Higginson, was wounded. Although the rescuers were unsuccessful in their efforts, the impact of this incident ". . . did more to crystallize Northern sentiment against slavery than any other except the exploit of John Brown, 'and this was the last time a fugitive slave was taken from Boston. It took 22 companies of state militia, four platoons of marines, a battalion of United States artillerymen, and the city's police force . . . to ensure the performance of this shameful act, the cost of which, to the Federal government alone, came to forty thousand dollars.' "[1]

Throughout the era of slavery, Blacks as well as progressive whites recurrently discovered that their commitment to the anti-slavery cause frequently entailed the overt violation of the laws of the land. Even as

[1] William Z. Foster, *The Negro People in American History,* International Publishers, New York, 1954, pp. 169–70 (quoting Herbert Aptheker).

slavery faded away into a more subtle yet equally pernicious apparatus to dominate Black people, "illegal" resistance was still on the agenda. After the Civil War, the Black Codes, successors to the old slave codes, legalized convict labor, prohibited social intercourse between Blacks and whites, gave white employers an excessive degree of control over the private lives of Black workers, and generally codified racism and terror. Naturally, numerous individual as well as collective acts of resistance prevailed. On many occasions, Blacks formed armed teams to protect themselves from white terrorists who were, in turn, protected by law enforcement agencies, if not actually identical with them.

By the second decade of the twentieth century, the mass movement, headed by Marcus Garvey, proclaimed in its Declaration of Rights that Black people should not hesitate to disobey all discriminatory laws. Moreover, the Declaration announced, they should utilize all means available to them, legal or illegal, to defend themselves from legalized terror as well as Ku Klux Klan violence. During the era of intense activity around civil rights issues, systematic disobedience of oppressive laws was a primary tactic. The sit-ins were organized transgressions of racist legislation.

All these historical instances involving the overt violation of the laws of the land converge around an unmistakable common denominator. At stake has been the collective welfare and survival of a people. There is a distinct and qualitative difference between one breaking a law for one's own individual self-interest and violating it in the interests of a class or a people whose oppression is expressed either directly or indirectly through that particular law. The former might be called a criminal (though in many instances he is a victim), but the latter, as a reformist or revolutionary, is interested in universal social change. Captured, he or she is a political prisoner.

The political prisoner's words or deeds have in one form or another embodied political protests against the established order and have consequently brought him into acute conflict with the state. In light of the political content of his act, the "crime" (which may or may not have been committed) assumes a minor importance. In this country, however, where the special category of political prisoners is not officially acknowledged, the political prisoner inevitably stands trial for a specific criminal offense, not for a political act. Often the so-called crime does not even have a nominal existence. As in the 1914 murder frame-up of the IWW organizer, Joe Hill, it is a blatant fabrication, a mere excuse for silencing a militant crusader against oppression. In all instances, however, the political prisoner has violated the unwritten law which prohibits disturbances and upheavals in the status quo of exploitation and racism. This unwritten law has been contested by actually and explicitly breaking a law or by utilizing constitutionally protected channels to educate, agitate and organize the masses to resist.

A deep-seated ambivalence has always characterized the official response to the political prisoner. Charged and tried for a criminal act, his guilt is always political in nature. This ambivalence is perhaps best captured by Judge Webster Thayer's comment upon sentencing Bartolomeo Vanzetti to 15 years for an attempted payroll robbery: "This man, although he may not have actually committed the crime attributed to him, is nevertheless morally culpable, because he is the enemy of our existing institutions." [2] (The very same judge, incidentally, sentenced Sacco and Vanzetti to death for a robbery and murder of which they were manifestly innocent.) It is not surprising that Nazi Germany's foremost constitutional lawyer, Carl Schmitt, advanced a theory which generalized this *a priori* culpability. A thief, for example, was not necessarily one who has committed an overt act of theft, but rather one whose character renders him a thief *(wer nach seinem wesen ein Dieb ist)*. Nixon's and J. Edgar Hoover's pronouncements lead one to believe that they would readily accept Schmitt's fascist legal theory. Anyone who seeks to overthrow oppressive institutions, whether or not he has engaged in an overt illegal act, is *a priori* a criminal who must be buried away in one of America's dungeons.

Even in all Martin Luther King's numerous arrests, he was not so much charged with the nominal crimes of trespassing, disturbance of the peace, etc., but rather with being an enemy of Southern society, an inveterate foe of racism. When Robert Williams was accused of a kidnapping, this charge never managed to conceal his real offense—the advocacy of Black people's incontestable right to bear arms in their own defense.

The offense of the political prisoner is his political boldness, his persistent challenging—legally or extra-legally—of fundamental social wrongs fostered and reinforced by the state. He has opposed unjust laws and exploitative, racist social conditions in general, with the ultimate aim of transforming these laws and this society into an

[2] Louis Adamic, *Dynamite: The History of Class Violence in America,* Peter Smith, Gloucester, Mass., 1963, p. 312.

order harmonious with the material and spiritual needs and interests of the vast majority of its members.

Nat Turner and John Brown were political prisoners in their time. The acts for which they were charged and subsequently hanged, were the practical extensions of their profound commitment to the abolition of slavery. They fearlessly bore the responsibility for their actions. The significance of their executions and the accompanying widespread repression did not lie so much in the fact that they were being punished for specific crimes, nor even in the effort to use their punishment as an implicit threat to deter others from similar *armed* acts of resistance. These executions and the surrounding repression of slaves were intended to terrorize the anti-slavery movement in general; to discourage and diminish both legal and illegal forms of abolitionist activity. As usual, the effect of repression was miscalculated and, in both instances, anti-slavery activity was accelerated and intensified as a result.

Nat Turner and John Brown can be viewed as examples of the political prisoner who has actually committed an act which is defined by the state as "criminal." They killed and were consequently tried for murder. But did they commit murder? This raises the question of whether American revolutionaries had *murdered* the British in their struggle for liberation. Nat Turner and his followers killed some 65 white people, yet shortly before the Revolt had begun, Nat is reputed to have said to the other rebelling slaves: "Remember that ours is not war for robbery nor to satisfy our passions, it is a *struggle for freedom.* Ours must be deeds not words." [3]

The very institutions which condemned Nat Turner and reduced his struggle for freedom to a simple criminal case of murder, owed their existence to the decision, made a half century earlier, to take up arms against the British oppressor.

The battle for the liquidation of slavery had no legitimate existence in the eyes of the government and therefore the special quality of deeds carried out in the interests of freedom was deliberately ignored. There were no political prisoners, there were only criminals; just as the movement out of which these deeds flowed was largely considered criminal.

Likewise, the significance of activities which are pursued in the interests of liberation today is minimized not so much because officials

[3] Herbert Aptheker, *Nat Turner's Slave Rebellion,* Grove Press, New York, 1968, p. 45. According to Aptheker these are not Nat Turner's exact words.

are unable to *see* the collective surge against oppression, but because they have consciously set out to subvert such movements. In the Spring of 1970, Los Angeles Panthers took up arms to defend themselves from an assault initiated by the local police force on their office and on their persons. They were charged with criminal assault. If one believed the official propaganda, they were bandits and rogues who pathologically found pleasure in attacking policemen. It was not mentioned that their community activities—educational work, services such as free breakfast and free medical programs—which had legitimized them in the Black community, were the immediate reason for which the wrath of the police had fallen upon them. In defending themselves from the attack waged by some 600 policemen (there were only 11 Panthers in the office) they were not only defending their lives, but even more important their accomplishments in the Black community surrounding them and in the broader thrust for Black Liberation. Whenever Blacks in struggle have recourse to self-defense, particularly armed self-defense, it is twisted and distorted on official levels and ultimately rendered synonymous with criminal aggression. On the other hand, when policemen are clearly indulging in acts of criminal aggression, officially they are defending themselves through "justifiable assault" or "justifiable homicide."

The ideological acrobatics characteristic of official attempts to explain away the existence of the political prisoner do not end with the equation of the individual political act with the individual criminal act. The political act is defined as criminal in order to discredit radical and revolutionary movements. A political event is reduced to a criminal event in order to affirm the absolute invulnerability of the existing order. In a revealing contradiction, the court resisted the description of the New York Panther 21 trial as "political," yet the prosecutor entered as evidence of criminal intent, literature which represented, so he purported, the political ideology of the Black Panther Party.

The legal apparatus designates the Black liberation fighter a criminal, prompting Nixon, Agnew, Reagan *et al.* to proceed to mystify with their demagogy millions of Americans whose senses have been dulled and whose critical powers have been eroded by the continual onslaught of racist ideology.

As the Black Liberation Movement and other progressive struggles increase in magnitude and intensity, the judicial system and its extension, the penal system, consequently become key weapons in the state's fight to preserve the existing conditions of class domination, therefore racism, poverty and war.

In 1951, W. E. B. Du Bois as Chairman of the Peace Information Center, was indicted by the Federal government for "failure to register as an agent of a foreign principle." In assessing this ordeal which occurred in the ninth decade of his life, he turned his attention to the inhabitants of the nation's jails and prisons:

> What turns me cold in all this experience is the certainty that thousands of innocent victims are in jail today because they had neither money nor friends to help them. The eyes of the world were on our trial despite the desperate efforts of press and radio to suppress the facts and cloud the real issues; the courage and money of friends and of strangers who dared stand for a principle freed me; but God only knows how many who were as innocent as I and my colleagues are today in hell. They daily stagger out of prison doors embittered, vengeful, hopeless, ruined. And of this army of the wronged, the proportion of Negroes is frightful. We protect and defend sensational cases where Negroes are involved. But the great mass of arrested or accused Black folk have no defense. There is desperate need of nationwide organizations to oppose this national racket of railroading to jails and chain gangs the poor, friendless and Black.[4]

Almost two decades passed before the realization attained by Du Bois on the occasion of his own encounter with the judicial system achieved extensive acceptance. A number of factors have combined to transform the penal system into a prominent terrain of struggle, both for the captives inside and the masses outside. The impact of large numbers of political prisoners both on prison populations and on the mass movement has been decisive. The vast majority of political prisoners have not allowed the fact of imprisonment to curtail their educational, agitational and organizing activities, which they continue behind prison walls. And in the course of developing mass movements around political prisoners, a great deal of attention has inevitably been focused on the institutions in which they are imprisoned. Furthermore the political receptivity of prisoners—especially Black and Brown captives—has been increased and sharpened by the surge of aggressive political activity rising out of Black, Chicano and other oppressed communities. Finally, a major catalyst for intensified political action in and around prisons has emerged out of the transformation of convicts, originally found guilty of criminal

[4] *Autobiography of W. E. B. Du Bois,* International Publishers, New York, 1968, p. 390.

offenses, into exemplary political militants. Their patient educational efforts in the realm of exposing the specific oppressive structures of the penal system in their relation to the larger oppression of the social system have had a profound effect on their fellow captives.

The prison is a key component of the State's coercive apparatus, the overriding function of which is to ensure social control. The etymology of the term "penitentiary" furnishes a clue to the controlling idea behind the "prison system" at its inception. The penitentiary was projected as the locale for doing penitence for an offense against society, the physical and spiritual purging of proclivities to challenge rules and regulations which command total obedience. While cloaking itself with the bourgeois aura of universality—imprisonment was supposed to cut across all class lines, as crimes were to be defined by the act, not the perpetrator—the prison has actually operated as an instrument of class domination, a means of prohibiting the have-nots from encroaching upon the haves.

The occurrence of crime is inevitable in a society in which wealth is unequally distributed, as one of the constant reminders that society's productive forces are being channeled in the wrong direction. The majority of criminal offenses bear a direct relationship to property. Contained in the very concept of property crimes are profound but suppressed social needs which express themselves in antisocial modes of action. Spontaneously producted by a capitalist organization of society, this type of crime is at once a protest against society and a desire to partake of its exploitative content. It challenges the symptoms of capitalism, but not its essence.

Some Marxists in recent years have tended to banish "criminals" and the lumpenproletariat as a whole from the arena of revolutionary struggle. Apart from the absence of any link binding the criminal to the means of production, underlying this exclusion has been the assumption that individuals who have recourse to antisocial acts are incapable of developing the discipline and collective orientation required by revolutionary struggle.

With the declassed character of lumpenproletarians in mind, Marx had stated that they are as capable of "the most heroic deeds and the most exalted sacrifices, as of the basest banditry and the dirtiest corruption."[5] He emphasized the fact that the Provisional Government's Mobile Guards under the Paris Commune—some 24,000 troops—were largely formed out of young lumpenproletarians from 15

[5] Karl Marx, "The Class Struggle in France," in *Handbook of Marxism,* International Publishers, New York, 1935, p. 109.

to 20 years of age. Too many Marxists have been inclined to overvalue the second part of Marx's observation—that the lumpenproletariat is capable of the basest banditry and the dirtiest corruption—while minimizing or indeed totally disregarding his first remark, applauding the lumpen for their heroic deeds and exalted sacrifices.

Especially today when so many Black, Chicano and Puerto Rican men and women are jobless as a consequence of the internal dynamic of the capitalist system, the role of the unemployed, which includes the lumpenproletariat, in revolutionary struggle must be given serious thought. Increased unemployment, particularly for the nationally oppressed, will continue to be an inevitable by-product of technological development. At least 30 percent of Black youth are presently without jobs. In the context of class exploitation and national oppression, it should be clear that numerous individuals are compelled to resort to criminal acts, not as a result of conscious choice—implying other alternatives—but because society has objectively reduced their possibilities of subsistence and survival to this level. This recognition should signal the urgent need to organize the unemployed and lumpenproletariat as indeed the Black Panther Party as well as activists in prison have already begun to do.

In evaluating the susceptibility of the Black and Brown unemployed to organizing efforts, the peculiar historical features of the United States, specifically racism and national oppression, must be taken into account. There already exists in the Black and Brown communities, the lumpenproletariat included, a long tradition of collective resistance to national oppression.

Moreover, in assessing the revolutionary potential of prisoners in America as a group, it should be borne in mind that not all prisoners have actually committed crimes. The built-in racism of the judicial system expresses itself, as Du Bois has suggested, in the railroading of countless innocent Blacks and other national minorities into the country's coercive institutions.

One must also appreciate the effects of disproportionally long prison terms on Black and Brown inmates. The typical criminal mentality sees imprisonment as a calculated risk for a particular criminal act. One's prison term is more or less rationally predictable. The function of racism in the judicial-penal complex is to shatter that predictability. The Black burglar, anticipating a 2- to 4-year term may end up doing 10 to 15 years, while the white burglar leaves after two years.

Within the contained, coercive universe of the prison, the captive is confronted with the realitites of racism, not simply as individual acts dictated by attitudinal bias; rather he is compelled to come to grips with racism as an institutional phenomenon collectively experienced by the victims. The disproportionate representation [in prisons] of the Black and Brown communities, the manifest racism of parole boards, the intense brutality inherent in the relationship between prison guards and Black and Brown inmates—all this and more cause the prisoner to be confronted daily, hourly, with the concentrated, systematic existence of racism.

For the innocent prisoner, the process of radicalization should come easy; for the "guilty" victim, the insight into the nature of racism as it manifests itself in the judicial-penal complex can lead to a questioning of his own past criminal activity and a re-evaluation of the methods he has used to survive in a racist and exploitative society. Needless to say, this process is not automatic, it does not occur spontaneously. The persistent educational work carried out by the prison's political activists plays a key role in developing the political potential of captive men and women.

Prisoners—especially Blacks, Chicanos, and Puerto Ricans—are increasingly advancing the proposition that they are *political* prisoners. They contend that they are political prisoners in the sense that they are largely the victims of an oppressive politico-economic order, swiftly becoming conscious of the causes underlying their victimization. The Folsom Prisoners' Manifesto of Demands and Anti-Oppression Platform attests to a lucid understanding of the structures of oppression within the prison—structures which contradict even the avowed function of the penal institution: "The program we are submitted to, under the ridiculous title of rehabilitation, is relative to the ancient stupidity of pouring water on the drowning man, in as much as we are treated for our hostilities by our program administrators with their hostility as medication." The Manifesto also reflects an awareness that the severe social crisis taking place in this country, predicated in part on the ever-increasing mass consciousness of deepening social contradictions, is forcing the political function of the prisons to surface in all its brutality. Their contention that prisons are being transformed into the "fascist concentration camps of modern America" should not be taken lightly, although it would be erroneous as well as defeatist in a practical sense, to maintain that fascism has irremediably established itself.

The point is this, and this is the truth which is apparent in the Manifesto: The ruling circles of America are expanding and intensifying repressive measures designed to nip revolutionary movements in the bud as well as to curtail radical-democratic tendencies, such as the movement to end the war in Indo-China. The government is not hesitating to utilize an entire network of fascist tactics, including the monitoring of congressmen's telephone calls, a system of "preventive fascism," as Marcuse has termed it, in which the role of the judicial and penal systems loom large. The sharp edge of political repression, cutting through the heightened militancy of the masses, and bringing growing numbers of activists behind prison walls, must necessarily pour over into the contained world of the prison where it understandably acquires far more ruthless forms.

It is a relatively easy matter to persecute the captive whose life is already dominated by a network of authoritarian mechanisms. This is especially facilitated by the indeterminate sentence policies of many states, for politically conscious prisoners will incur inordinately long sentences on their original conviction. According to Louis S. Nelson, warden of San Quentin Prison, ". . . if the prisons of California become known as 'schools for violent revolution,' the Adult Authority would be remiss in their duty not to keep the inmates longer" (San Francisco *Chronicle*, May 2, 1971). Where this is deemed inadequate, authorities have recourse to the whole spectrum of brutal corporal punishment, including out and out murder. At San Quentin, Fred Billingslea was teargassed to death in February, 1970. W. L. Nolan, Alvin Miller, and Cleveland Edwards were assassinated by a prison guard in January, 1970 at Soledad Prison. Unusual and inexplicable suicides have occurred with incredible regularity in jails and prisons throughout the country.

It should be self-evident that the frame-up becomes a powerful weapon within the spectrum of prison repression, particularly because of the availability of informers, the broken prisoners who will do anything for a price. The Soledad Brothers and the Soledad 3 are leading examples of frame-up victims. Both cases involve militant activists who have been charged with killing Soledad prison guards. In both cases, widespread support has been kindled within the California prison system. They have served as occasions to link the immediate needs of the Black community with a forceful fight to break the fascist stronghold in the prisons and therefore to abolish the prison system in its present form.

Racist oppression invades the lives of Black people on an infinite variety of levels. Blacks are imprisoned in a world where our labor and toil hardly allow us to eke out a decent existence, if we are able to find jobs at all. When the economy begins to falter, we are forever the first victims, always the most deeply wounded. When the economy is on its feet, we continue to live in a depressed state. Unemployment is generally twice as high in the ghettos as it is in the country as a whole and even higher among Black women and youth. The unemployment rate among Black youth has presently skyrocketed to 30 percent. If one-third of America's white youth were without a means of livelihood, we would either be in the thick of revolution or else under the iron rule of fascism. Substandard schools, medical care hardly fit for animals, overpriced, dilapidated housing, a welfare system based on a policy of skimpy concessions, designed to degrade and divide (and even this may soon be cancelled)—this is only the beginning of the list of props in the overall scenery of oppression which, for the mass of Blacks, is the universe.

In Black communities, wherever they are located, there exists an ever-present reminder that our universe must remain stable in its drabness, its poverty, its brutality. From Birmingham to Harlem to Watts, Black ghettos are occupied, patrolled and often attacked by massive deployments of police. The police, domestic caretakers of violence, are the oppressor's emissaries, charged with the task of containing us within the boundaries of our oppression.

The announced function of the police, "to protect and serve the people," becomes the grotesque caricature of protecting and preserving the interests of our oppressors and serving us nothing but injustice. They are there to intimidate Blacks, to persuade us with their violence that we are powerless to alter the conditions of our lives. Arrests are frequently based on whims. Bullets from their guns murder human beings with little or no pretext, aside from the universal intimidation they are charged with carrying out. Protection for drug-pushers, and Mafia-style exploiters, support for the most reactionary ideological elements of the Black community (especially those who cry out for more police), are among the many functions of forces of law and order. They encircle the community with a shield of violence, too often forcing the natural aggression of the Black community inwards. Fanon's analysis of the role of colonial police is an appropriate description of the function of the police in America's ghettos.

It goes without saying that the police would be unable to set into motion their racist machinery were they not sanctioned and supported by the judicial system. The courts not only consistently abstain from prosecuting criminal behavior on the part of the police, but they convict, on the basis of biased police testimony, countless Black men and women. Court-appointed attorneys, acting in the twisted interests of overcrowded courts, convince 85 percent of the defendants to plead guilty. Even the manifestly innocent are advised to cop a plea so that the lengthy and expensive process of jury trials is avoided. This is the structure of the apparatus which summarily railroads Black people into jails and prisons. (During my imprisonment in the New York Women's House of Detention, I encountered numerous cases involving innocent Black women who had been advised to plead guilty. One sister had entered her landlord's apartment for the purpose of paying rent. He attempted to rape her and in the course of the ensuing struggle, a lit candle toppled over, burning a tablecloth. The landlord ordered her arrested for arson. Following the advice of her court-appointed attorney, she entered a guilty plea, having been deceived by the attorney's insistence that the court would be more lenient. The sister was sentenced to three years.)

The vicious circle linking poverty, police, courts and prison is an integral element of ghetto existence. Unlike the mass of whites, the path which leads to jails and prisons is deeply rooted in the imposed patterns of Black existence. For this very reason, an almost instinctive affinity binds the mass of Black people to the political prisoners. The vast majority of Blacks harbor a deep hatred of the police and are not deluded by official proclamations of justice through the courts.

For the Black individual, contact with the law-enforcement-judicial-penal network directly or through relatives and friends, is inevitable because he is Black. For the activist become political prisoner, the contact has occurred because he has lodged a protest, in one form or another, against the conditions which nail Blacks to this orbit of oppression.

Historically, Black people as a group have exhibited a greater potential for resistance than any other part of the population. The ironclad rule over our communities, the institutional practice of genocide, the ideology of racism have performed a strictly political as well as an economic function. The capitalists have not only extracted super-profits from the underpaid labor of over 15 per cent of the American population with the aid of a superstructure of terror. This terror and more subtle forms of racism have further served to thwart the flowering of a resistance, even a revolution which would spread to the working class as a whole.

In the interests of the capitalist class, the consent to racism and terror has been demagogically elicited from the white population, workers included, in order to more efficiently stave off resistance.

Today, Nixon, Mitchell and J. Edgar Hoover are desperately attempting to persuade the population that dissidents, particularly Blacks, Chicanos, Puerto Ricans, must be punished for being members of revolutionary organizations; for advocating the overthrow of the government; for agitating and educating in the streets and behind prison walls. The political function of racist domination is surfacing with accelerated intensity. Whites, who have professed their solidarity with the Black Liberation Movement and have moved in a distinctly revolutionary direction, find themselves targets of the selfsame repression. Even the anti-war movement, rapidly exhibiting an anti-imperialist consciousness, is falling victim to government repression.

Black people are rushing full speed ahead toward an understanding of the circumstances which give rise to exaggerated forms of political repression and thus an overabundance of political prisoners. This understanding is being forged out of the raw material of their own immediate experiences with racism. Hence, the Black masses are growing conscious of their responsibility to defend those who are being persecuted for attempting to bring about the alleviation of the most injurious immediate problems facing Black communities and ultimately to bring about total liberation through armed revolution, if it must come to this.

The Black Liberation Movement is presently at a critical juncture. Fascist methods of repression threaten to physically decapitate and obliterate the movement. More subtle, yet not less dangerous ideological tendencies from within threaten to isolate the Black movement and diminish its revolutionary impact. Both menaces must be counteracted in order to ensure our survival. Revolutionary Blacks must spearhead and provide leadership for a broad anti-fascist movement.

Fascism is a process, its growth and development are cancerous in nature. While today, the threat of fascism may be primarily restricted to the use of the law-enforcement-judicial-penal apparatus to arrest the overt and latent-revolutionary trends among nationally oppressed people, tomorrow it may attack the working class en masse and eventually even moderate democrats. Even in this period, however, the cancer has already commenced to spread. In addition to the prison army of thousands and thousands of nameless Third World victims of political revenge, there are increasing numbers of white political prisoners—draft resisters, anti-war activists such as the Harrisburg 8, men and women who have involved themselves on all levels of revolutionary activity.

Among the further symptoms of the fascist threat are official efforts to curtail the power of organized labor, such as the attack on the manifestly conservative construction workers and the trends toward reduced welfare aid. Moreover, court decisions and repressive legislation augmenting police powers such as the Washington no-knock law, permitting police to enter private dwellings without warning and Nixon's "Crime Bill" in general—can eventually be used against any citizen. Indeed congressmen are already protesting the use of police-state wire-tapping to survey their activities. The fascist content of the ruthless aggression in Indo-China should be self-evident.

One of the fundamental historical lessons to be learned from past failures to prevent the rise of fascism is the decisive and indispensable character of the fight against fascism in its incipient phases. Once allowed to conquer ground, its growth is facilitated in geometric proportion. Although the most unbridled expressions of the fascist menace are still tied to the racist domination of Blacks, Chicanos, Puerto Ricans, Indians, it lurks under the surface wherever there is potential resistance to the power of monopoly capital, the parasitic interests which control this society. Potentially it can profoundly worsen the conditions of existence for the average American citizen. Consequently, the masses of people in this country have a real, direct and material stake in the struggle to free political prisoners, the struggle to abolish the prison system in its present form, the struggle against all dimensions of racism.

No one should fail to take heed of Georgi Dimitrov's warning: "Whoever does not fight the growth of fascism at these preparatory stages is not in a position to prevent the victory of fascism, but, on the contrary, facilitates that victory." (Report to the Seventh Congress of the Communist International, 1935.) The only effective guarantee against the victory of fascism is an indivisible mass movement which refuses to conduct business as usual as long as repression rages on. It is only natural that Blacks and other Third World peoples must lead this movement, for we are the first and most deeply injured victims and, most important, all working-class people, for the key to the triumph of fascism is its ideological victory over the entire working class. Given the eruption of a severe economic crisis, the door to such an ideological victory can be opened by the active approval or passive toleration of racism. It is essential that white workers become conscious that historically, through their acquiescence in the capitalist-inspired oppression of Blacks, they have only rendered themselves more vulnerable to attack.

The pivotal struggle which must be waged in the ranks of the working class is consequently the open, unreserved battle against entrenched racism. The white worker must become conscious of the threads which bind him to a James Johnson, Black auto worker, member of UAW, and a political prisoner presently facing charges for the killings of two foremen and a job setter. The merciless proliferation of the power of monopoly capital may ultimately push him inexorably down the very same path of desperation. No potential victim of the fascist terror should be without the knowledge that the greatest menace to racism and fascism is unity!

Marin County Jail
May, 1971

THE PANTHER 21: TO JUDGE MURTAGH

To: *"JUSTICE" MURTAGH*
From: *DEFENDANTS*

We the defendants named by the state in the proceedings now pending before "Justice" John M. Murtagh, in Part 38 Supreme Court, County of New York, say:

That the history of this nation has most definitely developed a dual set of social, economical and political realities, as well as dynamics. One white, and the other Black (the Black experience, or ghetto reality), having as their roots one of the most insidious and ruthless systems of human exploitation known to man, the enslavement and murder of over forty million Black people, spread over a period of less than three centuries.

Long ago in this nation certain basic decisions were made about Black people, but *not* consulting them. Even before the Constitution

From Robert Lefcourt, ed., *Law Against the People* (New York: Random House, Vintage Books, 1971:188–204). This letter was prepared entirely by the defendants in the within action, and transcribed, typed and reproduced with the help of their attorneys, due to their present incarceration.

was ever put on paper with its beautiful words and glowing rhetoric of man's equality and philosophical rights, human considerations had long given way before white economic necessity. Black people were to legally be defined and classified as nonhuman, below a horse—but definitely not a man.

Color became a crucial variable, and the foundation of the system of Black slavery. While chattel slavery is no longer upheld by the supreme law of the land, the habit and practice in thought and speech of looking at Black people from chattel plainly still persist. After much refinement, sophistication and development, it has remained to become imbedded in the national character, making itself clear in organized society, its institutions, and the attitudes of the dominant white culture to this very day.

For us to state there are two realities (experiences) that exist in this nation, is a statement of fact.

When we speak of American traditions, let us not forget the tradition of injustice inflicted again and again upon those [for] whom tradition has been created to exclude, exploit, dehumanize and murder.

Let us not conveniently forget how the system of "American justice" systematically upheld the bizarre reasoning about Black people in order to retain a system of slave labor. And when this became economically unnecessary, how "the great American system of justice" helped to establish and maintain social degradation and deprivation of all who were not white, and most certainly, those who were Black. To be sure, the entire country had to share in this denial; to justify the inhuman treatment of other human beings, the American had to conceal from himself and others his oppression of Blacks, but again the white dominant society has long had absolute power, especially over Black people—so it was no difficult matter to ignore them, define them, forget them, and if they persisted, pacify or punish them.

The duality of American society today need no longer be reinforced by laws, for it is now and has long been in the minds of men: the Harlems of America, as opposed to those who decide the fate of America's Harlems. This is essentially a historical continuation today, of yesterday—the plantation mentality, system and division, in the cloak of twentieth-century enlightenment.

"Traditional American justice," its very application has created what it claims to remedy, for its eyes are truly covered: it does not see the Black reality, nor does it consider or know of the Black experience, least of all consider it valid.

Black poor people are always subject to, but do not take part in your corrupt grand jury system and process.

We as a people do not exist except as victims, and to this and much more, we say no more. For 351½ years we said this in various ways. But running deep in the American psyche is the fear of the ex-slave. He who for so long has been wronged, will be wronged no more, and in fact will demand, fight and die for his human rights.

But why need we feel this way in the first place? Does not your Constitution guarantee man's freedom, his human dignity against state encroachment? Or does the innate fear of the rebellious slave in the heart of the slave-master continue to this day to negate all those guarantees in the cases of Black people? Does this cultural racist phobia make one forget, and abridge his own constitution, as this court has done to us? Do you not know what we mean when we say "NO MORE"? What has been done to us by your court, the district attorney, is only a reflection of all that has been infused into and permeates this racist society.

Black people have said and felt this for over 100 years. But those of the other reality, the dominant white culture, its institutions, had no ears to truly hear. The wax of centuries of slave-master–slave relationship had stopped up their ears, your ears. For if our reality, the Black experience in America, is invalid, then so are the institutions and social structure that contributed to its creation invalid. If you then concede it is valid (which it most definitely is), then it must be of consequence in determining what is "justice" compared to us (Black people).

White citizens have grown up with the identity of an American, and have enjoyed a completely different relationship to the institutions of this nation, with that, the unresolved conflicts of the ex-slaveholder.

Blacks are no longer the economic underpinning of the nation. But we continue to be willing, or unwilling, victims. There is a timeless quality to the unconscious which transforms yesterday into today.

On August 17, 1619, over a year prior to the landing of the pilgrims at Plymouth Rock, a Dutch privateer dropped anchor off Jamestown, Virginia. There she exchanged her cargo of twenty Black men, women, and children for provisions. According to the Dutch sailors, these Black people had been baptized, they were "Christians" and therefore could not be enslaved under British laws. As a result of that law, we were legally defined as "indentured" servants.

By 1663, though, the "Christian" conscience had given way to the capitalist desire for maximum profits. By 1663 the Carolinas and New

York, and Maryland in 1664, Delaware and Pennsylvania in 1682 perpetrated the most heinous and despicable act conceivable to the human mind, that of denying an entire race of people their freedom by relegating them to an eternal status of "chattel slavery" and this abominable feat was done through the courts, legally, and with the backing of guns—our first experience with "American justice."

But it did not stop there. Although later the "Declaration of Independence" proclaimed that "All men are created equal, that they are endowed by their creator with certain inalienable rights, that among these are Life, Liberty and the Pursuit of Happiness," there was a most interesting *omission.* In the original draft there was a paragraph that Thomas Jefferson intended to include in the list of grievances against King George III. The paragraph read: "He has waged cruel war against human nature itself, violating its most sacred rights of life and liberty in the person of a distant people (African, Black people), who never offended him; captivating and carrying them into slavery in another hemisphere, or to incur miserable death in their transportation thither."

This paragraph was omitted in the final document, and understandably. For not only would it have been a valid and factual indictment against King George, but also one against the "Founding Fathers" themselves.

When the "glorious" and "sacred" Constitution of the United States of America was drawn up in 1787, the "noble," "just" and "freedom-loving" men who had fought a long and bloody war against the tyrannical and oppressive British regime headed by King George, for their freedom, wrote into their constitution laws that further sanctified, legalized and protected that most "peculiar institution" (slavery). Apparently they recognized the absurd and repugnant contradiction, but not sufficiently enough to do anything other than exclude the term "Negro" and "slave" from that document.

The Constitution contained three provisions that dealt specifically with the issue of slavery. The first established the policy that in counting population in order to determine how many representatives a state might send to Congress all free persons and "three fifths of all other persons" were to be counted (Article I Sec. 2). The second forbade the Congress from making any laws restricting the slave trade until 1808 (Article I Sec. 9), and the third provided that runaway slaves who had escaped from any state had to be returned by any other state in which they might have sought refuge (Article IV Sec. 2).

The years passed and our wretched plight progressively worsened, the "laws" of bondage became even more institutionalized, inculcated in the dominant culture. In order to further protect and perpetuate their domination over us, the southern states passed many repressive laws called "slave codes." For us, there was not freedom of assembly. If more than four or five slaves came together without permission from a white person, the gathering in the depraved minds of the slave-masters was construed as a conspiracy. The towns and cities imposed a 9 P.M. curfew on us, there was no freedom of movement, a pass had to be carried by the slave whenever he was out of the presence of his master. And to enforce these ignoble laws there were slave patrols, organized like militias, composed of armed and mounted whites. (This mentality persists to this day. Woe to the Black man who is out very late in a white neighborhood; the police—white—suspect him immediately of being up to some foul deed. Even into the ghetto the white policeman brings this mentality.)

Although slavery had been abolished in certain states, the Black people who lived in those states were subjected to degrading laws which belied their so-called free status, and even worse, they were subject to kidnapping and being sold into slavery. The so-called free Black man was anything but free under the "American system of justice."

Throughout this horrid epoch, a few slaves managed to escape, then more slaves. The slaveholders demanded that the runaway slave laws be enforced. They pleaded to the United States Supreme Court, and that "august" body, the most powerful judiciary body in the land, the ultimate interpreter of the Constitution, answered their plea by upholding the 1793 Fugitive Slave Act in 1842, and again in 1845, and made it more stringent yet in 1850. Now for the runaway slave escaping to the North was not enough, for the Northern cities were overrun with slave-catchers.

In July 1847, Dred Scott, a Black resident of Missouri, brought suit in a Federal Court for his freedom. It read:

> Your petitioner, Dred Scott, a man of color, respectfully represents that sometime in the year of 1835 your petitioner was "purchased" as a slave by one John Emerson, since deceased, who . . . conveyed your petitioner from the state of Missouri to Fort Snelling (Illinois) a fort then occupied by the troops of the United States and under the jurisdiction of the United States.

In essence Dred Scott was claiming that since he had been

transported into territory (Illinois) in which slavery was forbidden by an act of Congress as well as state law, he was now a free man. This case was looked upon as a test to determine just what rights a Black man had in this country. It was the profound hope of many that a just and humane verdict would be rendered.

It took the Dred Scott case ten years to reach the "sacred" halls of the Supreme Court, and when that "prestigious" group of men spoke in March 1857 through the voice of "Chief Justice" Roger Taney, the Court ruled that "people of African descent are not and cannot be citizens of the United States and cannot sue in any court of the United States," and that Black people have "no rights which whites are bound to respect"—a classic example of the "American way of justice."

The Reconstruction Era was a time of great and unparalleled hope. It seemed as though Black people were finally to be accorded equal and humane treatment when the Thirteenth, Fourteenth, and Fifteenth Amendments were enacted.

But terror, violence, intimidation and murder still haunted us: the Ku Klux Klan did "their thing."

In 1866, 1871, and 1875 Congress enacted the first significant civil rights laws. They theoretically gave Black people the right to equal housing, accommodations, facilities and access to public transportation and places of public amusement. But as Blacks well know and whites deny, there is a world of difference in America between theory and practice. For although the Thirteenth, Fourteenth and Fifteenth Amendments and the civil rights legislation "gave" Black people so-called freedom, the right of citizenship and the right to vote, the enforcement of those laws was an entirely different thing. The extent of enforcement was totally dependent upon the degree to which it was advantageous to the Republican Party and the Northern industrialist.

By 1876 it was decided that Black people had served their purpose and, therefore, even the pretense of Black equality was no longer necessary.

The Supreme Court in 1883 embodied that attitude in law by declaring that the civil rights legislation of 1866, 1871, and 1875 was unconstitutional. In other decisions it displayed its remarkable and ingenious talent for interpreting the law according to the needs and interests of the dominant white ruling class. It nullified the Fourteenth and Fifteenth Amendments by declaring that they were Federal restrictions only on the powers of the states or their agents, not on the powers of individuals within those states. Thus it was still illegal for any states to violate or abridge the rights of Black people; but if on the other hand private citizens or a group of them (such as the Ku Klux Klan) within any state actively prevented Black people from exercising their rights, then the crime came under the jurisdiction of the state in which the crime, or crimes, took place.

The court also ruled that if a state law did not appear on its surface discriminatory against Black people, there the federal courts had no right to investigate. But this was not enough. It was necessary to go even further, and they did.

In 1896 the Supreme Court in *Plessy vs. Ferguson*, 163 U.S. 537, upheld a Louisiana law requiring segregated railroad facilities. As long as equality of accommodations existed, the court held segregation did not constitute discrimination, and Black people were not deprived of equal protection of the law under the Fourteenth Amendment. American justice!

Segregation automatically meant discrimination. Black people were forced to use in public buildings, freight elevators and toilet facilities reserved for janitors. On trains, all Black people, even those with first-class tickets, were forced to seat themselves in the baggage car. Employment discrimination and wage discrimination, "inferior" schools for Black children. All of these inhuman crimes were made legal by the highest court in the land. Typical American justice, for Black people.

In 1954, only after intense domestic pressure and international unveiling as a nation of hypocrites, the Supreme Court reversed the infamous *Plessy vs. Ferguson* decision and ruled that segregated educational facilities were unconstitutional. But this ruling, like virtually every seemingly just decision for Black people, was almost immediately revealed as a sham, a mere gesture to pacify us and alleviate your embarrassment. For the public schools of the nation are still overwhelmingly segregated and unequal, the result of a century of duality.

In the North, in the South, in the East and in the West, all over the country, Black people are accused of crimes, thrown in your jails, dragged through your courts and administered a sour dose of "American justice." We are in jail outside, and in jail inside. Black people and now all poor people have been well educated in the American system of justice.

We know very well what is meant by your statement, "This court is responsible for maintaining proper respect for the administration of criminal justice and preventing any reflection on the image of

American justice." Properly translated, it simply means that the farce must go on. The image must remain intact.

It is precisely these contradictions—of maintaining justice as a reality or rhetorically asserting such procedure—that must be resolved. The process of judicial determination by which the legal rights of private parties or the people are vindicated and the guilt or innocence of accused persons is established has a history that is as variable as the color and the class of the individual prosecuted. It is not only doubtful, it is appalling, to say the least.

Accusations of contempt for the "dignity" of and lack of respect for the court indicate to us, the defendants, that a devious attempt by the court prevails to obscure the truth of these proceedings. There is a glaring distinction between theory and practice within the "halls of justice" which is consistent with judicial history as it pertains to Black and poor people. This is why the brief history. What fool cannot see that the "justice" of which you speak has a dual interpretation quite apart from the legal definition and is in keeping with "slave-master" traditions?

In light of historical fact, we must put into the proper perspective, context, and true time continuum the question as to whether justice and United States constitutional rights are effectively afforded unvaryingly to all who stand before the "American system" of justice, that exercises due process.

Just law, in reality, shall not be defamed by its dual application according to racial and social values because of wealth, position and influence. History provides doubt of the "American system" of justice when comparison of class orientation defines the degree of rights, respect and justice the individual shall receive. Political favor for judicial position has not varied even to the present.

With such political relationships existing, have the courts, in practice, escaped from the abuse of authority which is a threat to the development of a free nation of people? Fascism encroaches in just such a manner. Historically the qualitative change in society still reveals a lack of humane interaction with the social, economically and politically exploited and isolated Black and poor peoples. The preceding chronology substantiates a blatant contempt for Black people and other non-white poor people, not recognizing their human rights and liberties as a matter of law, or morality, and substantiates a total disregard to our social reality, and is an insult to us. We can see the yesterday in today, and the history of our particular case runs upon the same tracks as does our people's long struggle.

This court represents the most ruthless system in the world, caring nothing for the wholesale misery that it brings, while at the same time your papers are full of verbiage of your "nobility," "righteousness," "justice," "fairness," and the "good" that you do.

We are very, very sick and tired of the BIG LIE. We cannot stand passive to the big lie any longer. We cannot accept it any longer.

It is time to state the truth, for Black people, for poor Puerto Rican, Mexican American, Chinese American, Indian and poor white people. The "Amerikkan system of justice" is a hideous sham and a revolting farce.

We must look at the situation objectively. As has been implied in the preceding, we realize that we are not second-class citizens at all. We are a colonized people. (Read your own Commission Reports.) We see that we are still considered chattel. We see how the Fugitive Slave Act has been modified in words, but is still being used, how the Dred Scott decision was never really reversed. That the Thirteenth, Fourteenth and Fifteenth Amendments of the Constitution did not liberate us—that in fact, in social reality, they only legalized slavery and expanded the Dred Scott decision to include Indians, Spanish-speaking and poor white people.

We see that things have not gotten better, but only progressively worse, and that includes tyranny. We completely oppose racism and tyranny and will continue to do so. You wish us to act according to a decorum set down by an organization, the "American Bar Association," which is not only racist, but is also not against genocide. (Perhaps they realize the truth, and see that the American ruling class is definitely liable for its treatment of Black people?)

In court you ask us to submit to a code of laws . . . your laws, not our laws (Black and poor people) but *your* laws—your laws because we were never asked (Black people) if we consented to having them as our laws, nor are these laws relevant to our ghetto reality. They are *your* laws, and we find them racist and oppressive. They, these laws, perpetuate our plantation continuation. Right now, in 1970, ninety percent of the inmates of your prisons are non-white. Ninety percent! And we (Black people, etc.) have never had the right to decide if we wanted to be governed by laws which we had no part in making. Yet, the primary concern of the men who drafted the "Declaration of Independence" was the *consent* of the governed by laws which they had a part in forming and which were relevant to them. We are in your prison, but these are not our laws. They are your laws, and in dealing with Black and poor people, you do not even adhere to *your own laws*.

In fact, a leading criminologist, Dr. R. R. Korn of Stanford University, has noted that eighty percent of the people now in prison were put there *illegally* according to *your* own law. (Strange that the overwhelming population is Black and non-white?)

Mr. Murtagh—your record speaks for itself. You are known in the ghetto as a "hanging judge." (How many Black and white poor men did you convict without their even having counsel just in 1969 alone, in your clever slick way?) Frank Hogan and his aides are well known—very well known in the ghetto—known for what they are—racist and unethical. (We have knowledge of cases, since our incarceration, of assistant district attorneys or D.A.'s men posing as legal aides to get conviction.) But in our case you and Mr. Hogan have gotten together and have outdone yourselves in denying us *all*, every one of our "alleged" state, federal and human rights. The record clearly shows this, when not clouded with the mist of racism.

A) Let us clear up one basic misconception. You constantly refer to this case as a "criminal" trial, while all of the time we *know,* you *know,* Frank Hogan knows, the people know, the other prisoners and even the guards know that this is *not* a criminal trial. Everyone knows that this is a political trial, for if we were not members of the Black Panther Party, a lot of things would never have been done to us in the first place.

Why are we not allowed to be with other prisoners? Why are we not allowed to even talk to the other prisoners? Why are we isolated? (Something we might say or do that can open their eyes, perhaps?) Alleged murderers and rapists are not treated in this manner, even "convicted" murderers and rapists are not treated in the manner in which we were treated. Why do you persist in the big lie? It is one of many clear contradictions.

(B) On April 2, 1969, hordes of "police" broke down our doors or otherwise forced entry into our homes, and ran amok. Rampaging and rummaging through our homes, they seized articles from us with wild abandon while having no search warrants. The "police" put us and our families in grave danger, nervously aiming shotguns, rifles and pistols at us and our families—even our children.

We were then kidnapped, as were some of our families. We state "kidnap" because many of us were never shown any arrest warrant, even to this day. This is illegal. This is a blatant contradiction of your own Constitution. . . . We said nothing.

(C) Upon the arrest of *some* of the defendants and before the appearance of any of the defendants, New York City district attorney

Frank Hogan appeared on national radio and national television (channels 2, 4, 5, 7, 9, and 11) in a press conference, during which time he gave out information from an "indictment" against us in an inflammatory and provocative manner, deliberately designed to incite the people against us and to deny us even the semblance of a "fair trial." Mr. Hogan implied a lie—that we had been seized on the way to commit these alleged acts with bombs in our hands—rather than the truth—that we had no bombs and that most of us were taken out of our beds.

Subsequent to that press conference, "unidentified police sources" and "persons close to the investigation" stated falsely to the press that we, as members of the Black Panther Party, were being aided and abetted by foreign governments considered hostile to your government (*i.e.,* Cuba and China)—that we, as Black Panther Party members, were stealing money from federal and/or state agencies and many other false, wild charges designed to heighten the public alarm against us and our Party, rather than diminish it, so as to create an atmosphere conducive to the extermination of the Black Panther Party and justify anything that might be done to us.

This unethical behavior gave, aided, and abetted further prejudicial pre-trial publicity, in direct contradiction to your law as outlined in the Fourteenth Amendment of your Constitution of the United States. Due to this behavior alone, we are positive that we could not get a fair trial anywhere in this country. . . . We still said nothing.

(D) When our attorneys learned of our arrest, they attempted to see us, as we were being held in your district attorney's office. They were refused permission to do so. At the "arraignment" a similar request by our counsel was again refused by Mr. Charles Marks, who presided thereat. These refusals were in blatant violation of your law as outlined in the Sixth and Fourteenth amendments of your Constitution of the United States . . . We continued to be silent.

(E) At this "arraignment" this Mr. Charles Marks, who was presiding, refused to read, explain or give us a copy of this "indictment" against us. This is another violation of your law as outlined in the Sixth and Fourteenth amendments of your Constitution of the United States . . . We remained silent.

(F) Bail (ransom) was set at $100,000, which is ridiculous and tantamount to no bail at all. This is another violation of your own law as outlined in the Eighth and Fourteenth amendments of your Constitution of the United States. We state that this bail is not only contradictory to your own law, but that it is also racist. When white "radical" groups are arrested, their bails do not usually exceed $10,000. When three Yemenites were charged with "conspiracy" to murder your President Nixon, and with the equipment to do such, their bail was $25,000; when Minutemen in New York were arrested and charged with a conspiracy to commit murder, the murder of 155 persons, and were arrested with more than enough bombs and guns to do this, bail was set at $25,000. We had no bombs. Our bail was $100,000 . . . We remained silent.

(G) At this arraignment, this Mr. Charles Marks, the same "judge" who is alleged to have signed the "arrest warrants," stated in words or substance that he was accepting all of the allegations in the "indictment" against us to be true. On subsequent hearings during April and May 1969, concerning reduction of ransom (bail), at which this same Mr. Marks still presided, he stated that we were "un-American" and that the law "did not apply to us" (sounds of history?). This does not quite show impartiality . . . Yet, we said nothing.

(H) Our counsel have been in front of at least 35 "judges" concerning our bail, and this attitude permeates the "great American system of justice." All motions on this were denied, either without comment or because of the "seriousness" of the "charges" but *never* dealing with the constitutional issues involved, and it is *your* Constitution. All of this seems to underlie "judge" Marks's remarks . . . Yet, we said nothing.

(I) We have been treated like animals—in fact, like less than animals. On January 17, 1969, Miss Joan Bird was kidnapped, beaten, and tortured. She was punched and beaten, given the "thumb torture," hung upside down by the ankle from out of a third-story window of a "Police Precinct." On April 2–3, 1969, some of us were beaten as we were being kidnapped. From April 2, 1969, all of us were placed under constant abuse and harassment, which included 24-hour lock-in, complete isolation, no library or recreation, lights kept on in our cells for 24 hours, physical assaults, deprivations of seeing our families, at times denied mattresses, medication, sheets, showers, pillow-cases, towels, soap, toothpaste, and toilet paper.

Our families have suffered abuse in visiting us, and mental anguish. One of us suffered the loss of a child because of this. Some of our families had to go on welfare because of our outrageous incarceration and ransom. We were denied mail, even from our attorneys—denied access to consult all together with our attorneys. We have been subjected to the most onerous and barbaric of jail conditions. The objective of all this was our psychological and physical destruction during our pre-trial detention.

As *Newsweek* Magazine even states, ". . . the handling of the suspects between their arrest and their trial was something less than a model of American criminal justice," and "none of it was very becoming to the state." (How well we know.) All this is a blatant violation of your own law as outlined in the Eighth and Fourteenth Amendments of your own Federal Constitution . . . Yet, we *still* remained silent.

(J) You—Murtagh. You came into the case in May 1969. You were informed of these conditions. You could have righted these blatant violations of your own law, the laws you have "sworn" to uphold. But you did not. You refused to do this . . . and remained silent. You tried to rush us pell-mell to trial, knowing full well that we were not, could not, be prepared. . . . We remained silent.

We filed motions that are guaranteed to "citizens" by the Fourteenth Amendment of your Federal Constitution. You denied them all. You denied us the right, as guaranteed in your laws in the Sixth and Fourteenth amendments of your own Constitution, to conduct a *voir dire* of the grand jury in these proceedings, knowing full well that they did not comprise members of our peer group. . . . We remained silent.

You denied us a hearing with which to be confronted with the witnesses against us, as is guaranteed by your law in the Sixth Amendment of your Constitution. . . . We remained silent.

You denied us a Bill of Particulars, which is guaranteed by your laws in the Sixth and Fourteenth amendments of your Constitution. . . . We remained silent.

Two "suspects" were kidnapped under the modification of the Fugitive Slave Act in November 1969. You gave them no bail. (No sense pretending anymore, it seems.). . . . We remained silent.

You denied us every state and federal constitutional right, and remained silent. You substantiated Mr. Mark's "the law does not apply" to us. . . . Yet, we remained silent.

(K) Lee Berry. Lee Berry is a classical example of how you and your cohorts conduct the "American System of Justice" when dealing with Black people. On April 3, 1969, Lee Berry was a patient in the Veterans' Administration Hospital where he was receiving treatment as an epileptic, subject to Grand Mal seizures, which can be fatal. Lee Berry is not mentioned particularly in the "indictment." Yet, on April

3, 1969, your "police" dragged him out of the hospital. These "police" stood him up before your cohort, "judge" Marks. Lee was "arraigned" without counsel. Bail $100,000. He was thrown into an isolation cell in the Tombs without even a mattress. In July 1969, he was physically attacked without provocation and without warning, while he was in a drugged stupor.

You were aware of his condition—you were quite aware. Numerous motions were in your "Great Court System." It took four months to even get him medication, and only in November when he had become so ill, so progressively worse that it was frightening. He finally got consent to be transferred to Bellevue Hospital. Because of the court's decisions under your "American System of Justice," Lee Berry has had four serious operations within the last two months. Because of the court's decisions under the great American System of Justice at this precise moment Lee Berry is lying in the shadow of Death with a possible fatal case of pneumonia. At the very least, your Great Court System is guilty of attempted murder, and D.A. Hogan should be named as a co-defendant. Lee Berry is our Brother, and what is done to him has been done to us all . . . and we remained silent.

(L) In November 1969, four white persons were arrested for allegedly "bombing" various sites in New York City. They were arrested allegedly with "bombs in their possession," but they were white. For three of them, bail was reduced eighty percent in two days, because "the presumption of innocence is basic among both the statutory and constitutional principles affecting bail" . . . if you are white. (The political climate is such today, even this hardly matters any more if one is dissident.)

Two days after that decision, we were brought in front of you and given a superseding "indictment." We could be silent no longer. We had been insulted enough—more than enough. We had been treated with contempt in an atmosphere of intimidation for too long.

We must reiterate—we are looking at the situation objectively. Objective reality.

At the pre-trial hearings we are confronted with a "judge" who has admitted, in fact been indicted and arrested for ignoring "police" graft and corruption . . . a "judge" who by his record shows an unblemished career of "police" favoritism and all-American racism. In your previous dealings with Black people, you have shown yourself to be totally unjust, bloodthirsty, pitiless, and inhuman. We are confronted with a district attorney machine which has shown itself to be vigilant and unswerving in its racist policies. Ninety percent of the inmates convicted are nonwhite and poor. This machine has shown itself to be unethical in its techniques and practices—even in front of our eyes—tactics which include going up to and whispering to the witnesses on the stand, signalling and coaching them. We know, as *Look* Magazine stated in June 1969, "how the police corrupt the truth. . . . Prosecutors and judges become their accomplices." To cite a small example: A man, a Black man, was beaten to death in the Tombs in front of forty witnesses in May 1969 and the police swore that he died of a "heart attack." Yes, we *know* what the police will swear to. All Black people, poor people, know what the police will swear to. With all this, together with the hostility inculcated in the dominant white culture towards anything Black, is shown by you and your cohorts very well indeed. Under these conditions, and considering our stand on American racism, this is not only a challenge to us and Black people, but the whole people. To relate in terms you can understand, which Racist Woodrow Wilson stated (concerning fascism): "This is a challenge to all mankind; there is one choice we cannot make, we are incapable of making, we will not choose the path of submission . . . we will be, we must be as harsh as the Truth and as uncompromising as Justice—true Justice—is on our side." To that we say, Right On!

You have implied contempt charges. We cannot conceive of how this could be possible. How can we be in contempt of a court that is in contempt of its own laws? How can you be responsible for "maintaining respect and dispensing justice," when you have dispensed with justice, and you do not maintain respect for your own Constitution? How can you expect us to respect your laws, when you do not respect them yourself? Then you have the audacity to demand respect, when you, your whole Great System of Justice is out of order and does not respect us, or our rights.

You have talked about our counsel inciting us. Nothing could be further from the truth. The injustices we have been accorded over the past year incite us, the injustice in these hearings incites us, racism incites us, fascism incites us, in short—when we reflect back over history, its continuation up until today, you and your courts incite us.

But we will not leave it there for you and others, to distort, as some are inclined to do. There will be left no room for your courts and media to distort and misinterpret our actions. We wish for a speedy and FAIR trial, a just trial. But—we must have our alleged constitutional rights. This court is in contempt of our constitutional rights and has been for almost a year. We must have our rights first.

The wrongs inflicted must be redressed. Bygones are *not* bygones. Later for that. Three hundred and fifty-one and one-half years are enough. We must clean the slate. We do not believe in your appeals courts (we've had experience with 300 years of appeals generally, and thirty-five judges specifically). So we must begin with a mutual understanding anew. When we have our constitutional guarantees redressed, we will give the court the respect it claims to deserve—precisely the respect it deserves.

In light of all that has been said, in view of the collusion of the federal, state, and city courts, the New York City Department of Correction, the city police, and district attorney's office, we feel that we, as members of the Black Panther Party, cannot receive a fair and impartial trial without certain pre-conditions conforming to our alleged constitutional rights. So we state the following: we feel that the courts should follow their own federal Constitution, and when they have failed to do so, and continue to ignore their mistakes, but persist dogmatically to add insult to injury, those courts are in contempt of the people. One need not be black to relate to that, but it is often those who never experience such actions on the part of the courts who believe they, the courts, can never be wrong.

So, in keeping with that, and the social reality to which that principle must relate, we further state:

(1) That we have a constitutional right to reasonable bail, and that a few of us would, if they were white, be released in their own custody. We demand that right, and the court's consistent denial of that right in effect is in contempt of its own Constitution.

(2) We demand a jury of our peers, or people from our own community, as defined by the Constitution.

(3) We say that because the grand jury system in New York City systematically excludes poor Black people, it cannot be representative of a cross-section of the community from which we come. So in effect it is unconstitutional, and nothing more than a method of wielding class power and racial suppression and repression. We demand to have a constitutional and legal indictment, or be released, for we are being held illegally, by malicious and racist unethical laws.

(4) We demand that the unethical practice of the police and D.A.'s office in their production of evidence, lying, and misrepresentation, be strictly limited by the introduction of an impartial jury of our peers for all pre-trial hearings, to judge all motions and evidence submitted, subsequent to a new constitutional indictment.

Therefore, since you have effectively denied by your ruling of Wednesday, February 25, 1970, our right to a trial, and since this ruling will affect the future of Black and white political prisoners, we have directed our attorneys to do everything in their power to upset this vicious, barbaric, insidious and racist ruling, which runs head-on in contrast with the promise of the Thirteenth and Fourteenth Amendments of your U.S. Constitution.

Let this be entered into all records pertaining to our case.

All power to the people!

Lumumba Abdul Shakur
Richard Moore (Analye Dharuba)
Curtis Powell
Michael Tabor (Cetewayo)
Robert Collier
Walter Johnson (Baba Odinga)
Afeni Shakur
John J. Casson (Ali Bey Hassan)
Alex McKiever (Catarra)
Clark Squire
Joan Bird
Lee Roper
William King (Kinshasa)

DOMESTIC LAW AND INTERNATIONAL ORDER

ELDRIDGE CLEAVER

The police department and the armed forces are the two arms of the power structure, the muscles of control and enforcement. They have deadly weapons with which to inflict pain on the human body. They know how to bring about horrible deaths. They have clubs with which to bring about horrible deaths. They have clubs with which to beat the body and the head. They have bullets and guns with which to tear holes in the flesh, to smash bones, to disable and kill. They use force, to make you do what the deciders have decided you must do.

Every country on earth has these agencies of force. The people

From *Soul on Ice*, pp. 128–37, by Eldridge Cleaver.

everywhere fear this terror and force. To them it is like a snarling wild beast which can put an end to one's dreams. They punish. They have cells and prisons to lock you up in. They pass out sentences. They won't let you go when you want to. You have to stay put until they give the word. If your mother is dying, you can't go to her bedside to say goodbye or to her graveside to see her lowered into the earth, to see her, for the last time, swallowed up by that black hole.

The techniques of the enforcers are many: firing squads, gas chambers, electric chairs, torture chambers, the garrote, the guillotine, the tightening rope around your throat. It has been found that the death penalty is necessary to back up the law, to make it easier to enforce, to deter transgressions against the penal code. That everybody doesn't believe in the same laws is beside the point.

Which laws get enforced depends on who is in power. If the capitalists are in power, they enforce laws designed to protect their system, their way of life. They have a particular abhorrence for crimes against property, but are prepared to be liberal and show a modicum of compassion for crimes against the person—unless, of course, an instance of the latter is combined with an instance of the former. In such cases, nothing can stop them from throwing the whole book at the offender. For instance, armed robbery with violence, to a capitalist, is the very epitome of evil. Ask any banker what he thinks of it.

If Communists are in power, they enforce laws designed to protect their system, their way of life. To them, the horror of horrors is the speculator, that man of magic who has mastered the art of getting something with nothing and who in America would be a member in good standing of his local Chamber of Commerce.

"The people," however, are nowhere consulted, although everywhere everything is done always in their name and ostensibly for their betterment, while their real-life problems go unsolved. "The people" are a rubber stamp for the crafty and sly. And no problem can be solved without taking the police department and the armed forces into account. Both kings and bookies understand this, as do first ladies and common prostitutes.

The police do on the domestic level what the armed forces do on the international level: protect the way of life of those in power. The police patrol the city, cordon off communities, blockade neighborhoods, invade homes, search for that which is hidden. The armed forces patrol the world, invade countries and continents, cordon off nations, blockade islands and whole peoples; they will also overrun villages, neighborhoods, enter homes, huts, caves, searching for that which is hidden. The policeman and the soldier will violate your person, smoke you out with various gases. Each will shoot you, beat your head and body with sticks and clubs, with rifle butts, run you through with bayonets, shoot holes in your flesh, kill you. They each have unlimited firepower. They will use all that is necessary to bring you to your knees. They won't take no for an answer. If you resist their sticks, they draw their guns. If you resist their guns, they call for reinforcements with bigger guns. Eventually they will come in tanks, in jets, in ships. They will not rest until you surrender or are killed. The policeman and the soldier will have the last word.

Both police and the armed forces follow orders. Orders. Orders flow from the top down. Up there, behind closed doors, in antechambers, in conference rooms, gavels bang on the tables, the tinkling of silver decanters can be heard as icewater is poured by well-fed, conservatively dressed men in hornrimmed glasses, fashionably dressed American widows with rejuvenated faces and tinted hair, the air permeated with the square humor of Bob Hope jokes. Here all the talking is done, all the thinking, all the deciding. Gray rabbits of men scurry forth from the conference room to spread the decisions throughout the city, as News. Carrying out orders is a job, a way of meeting the payments on the house, a way of providing for one's kiddies. In the armed forces it is also a duty, patriotism. Not to do so is treason.

Every city has its police department. No city would be complete without one. It would be sheer madness to try operating an American city without the heat, the fuzz, the man. Americans are too far gone, or else they haven't arrived yet; the center does not exist, only the extremes. Take away the cops and Americans would have a coast-to-coast free-for-all. There are, of course, a few citizens who carry their own private cops around with them, built into their souls. But there is robbery in the land, and larceny, murder, rape, burglary, theft, swindles, all brands of crime, profit, rent, interest—and these blasé descendants of Pilgrims are at each other's throats. To complicate matters, there are also rich people and poor people in America. There are Negroes and whites, Indians, Puerto Ricans, Mexicans, Jews, Chinese, Arabs, Japanese—all with equal rights but unequal possessions. Some are haves and some are have-nots. All have been taught to worship at the throne of General Motors. The whites are on top in America and they want to stay there, up there. They are also on top in the world, on the international level, and they want to stay up there, too. Everywhere there are those who want to smash this precious toy clock of a system, they want ever so much to change it, to rearrange things, to pull the whites down off their high horse and make them equal. Everywhere the whites are fighting to prolong their status, to retard the erosion of their position. In America, when everything else fails, they call out the police. On the international level, when everything else fails, they call out the armed forces.

A strange thing happened in Watts, in 1965, August. The Blacks, who in this land of private property have all private and no property, got excited into an uproar because they noticed a cop before he had a chance to wash the blood off his hands. Usually the police department can handle such flare-ups. But this time it was different. Things got out of hand. The blacks were running amok, burning, shooting, breaking. The police department was powerless to control them; the chief called for reinforcements. Out came the National Guard, that ambiguous hybrid from the twilight zone where the domestic army merges with the international; that hypocritical force poised within America and capable of action on either level, capable of backing up either the police or the armed forces. Unleashing their formidable firepower, they crushed the blacks. But things will never be the same again. Too many people saw that those who turned the other cheek in Watts got their whole head blown off. At the same time, heads were being blown off in Vietnam. America was embarrassed, not by the quality of her deeds but by the surplus of publicity focused upon her negative selling points, and a little frightened because of what all those dead bodies, on two fronts, implied. Those corpses spoke eloquently of potential allies and alliances. A community of interest began to emerge, dripping with blood, out of the ashes of Watts. The blacks in Watts and all over America could now see the Viet Cong's point: both were on the receiving end of what the armed forces were dishing out.

So now the blacks, stung by the new knowledge they have unearthed, cry out: "POLICE BRUTALITY!" From one end of the country to the other, the new war cry is raised. The youth, those nodes of compulsive energy who are all fuel and muscle, race their motors, itch to do something. The Uncle Toms, no longer willing to get down on their knees to lick boots, do so from a squatting position. The black bourgeoisie call for Citizens' Review Boards, to assert civilian control over the activity of the police. In back rooms, in dark stinking corners of the ghettos, self-conscious black men curse their own cowardice and stare at their rifles and pistols and shotguns laid out on tables before them, trembling as they wish for a manly impulse to course through their bodies and send them screaming mad into the streets shooting from the hip. Black women look at their men as if they are bugs, curious growths of flesh playing an inscrutable waiting game. Violence becomes a homing pigeon floating through the ghettos seeking a black brain in which to roost for a season.

In their rage against the police, against police brutality, the blacks lose sight of the fundamental reality: that the police are only an instrument for the implementation of the policies of those who make the decisions. Police brutality is only one facet of the crystal of terror and oppression. Behind police brutality there is social brutality, economic brutality, and political brutality. From the perspective of the ghetto, this is not easy to discern: the TV newscaster and the radio announcer and the editorialists of the newspapers are wizards of the smoke screen and the snow job.

What is true on the international level is true also at home; except that the ace up the sleeve is easier to detect in the international arena. Who would maintain that American soldiers are in Vietnam on their own motion? They were conscripted into the armed forces and taught the wisdom of obeying orders. They were sent to Vietnam by orders of the generals in the Pentagon, who receive them from the Secretary of Defense, who receives them from the President, who is shrouded in mystery. The soldier in the field in Vietnam, the man who lies in the grass and squeezes the trigger when a little half-starved, trembling Vietnamese peasant crosses his sights, is only following orders, carrying out a policy and a plan. He hardly knows what it is all about. They have him wired-up tight with the slogans of TV and the World Series. All he knows is that he has been assigned to carry out a certain ritual of duties. He is well trained and does the best he can. He does a good job. He may want to please those above him with the quality of his performance. He may want to make sergeant, or better. This man is from some hicky farm in Shit Creek, Georgia. He only knew whom to kill after passing through boot camp. He could just as well come out ready to kill Swedes. He will kill a Swede dead, if he is ordered to do so.

Same for the policeman in Watts. He is not there on his own. They have all been assigned. They have been told what to do and what not to do. They have also been told what they better not do. So when they continually do something, in every filthy ghetto in this shitty land, it means only that they are following orders.

It's no secret that in America the blacks are in total rebellion against the System. They want to get their nuts out of the sand. They don't like the way America is run, from top to bottom. In America, everything is owned. Everything is held as private property. Someone has a brand on everything. There is nothing left over. Until recently, the blacks themselves were counted as part of somebody's private property, along with the chickens and goats. The blacks have not forgotten this, principally because they are still treated as if they are part of someone's inventory of assets—or perhaps, in this day of rage against the costs of welfare, blacks are listed among the nation's liabilities. On any account, however, blacks are in no position to respect or help maintain the institution of private property. What they want is to figure out a way to get some of that property for themselves, to divert it to their own needs. This is what it is all about, and this is the real brutality involved. This is the source of all brutality.

The police are the armed guardians of the social order. The blacks are the chief domestic victims of the American social order. A conflict of interest exists, therefore, between the blacks and the police. It is not solely a matter of trigger-happy cops, of brutal cops who love to crack black heads. Mostly it's a job to them. It pays good. And there are numerous fringe benefits. The real problem is a trigger-happy social order.

The Utopians speak of a day when there will be no police. There will be nothing for them to do. Every man will do his duty, will respect the rights of his neighbor, will not disturb the peace. The needs of all will be taken care of. Everyone will have sympathy for his fellow man. There will be no such thing as crime. There will be, of course, no prisons. No electric chairs, no gas chambers. The hangman's rope will be the thing of the past. The entire earth will be a land of plenty. There will be no crimes against property, no speculation.

It is easy to see that we are not on the verge of entering Utopia: there are cops everywhere. North and South, the Negroes are the have-nots. They see property all around them, property that is owned by whites. In this regard, the black bourgeoisie has become nothing but a ridiculous nuisance. Having waged a battle for entrance into the American mainstream continually for fifty years, all of the black bourgeoisie's defenses are directed outward, against the whites. They have no defenses against the blacks and no time to erect any. The black masses can handle them any time they choose, with one mighty blow. But the white bourgeoisie presents a bigger problem, those whites who own everything. With many shackled by unemployment, hatred in black hearts for this system of private property increases daily. The sanctity surrounding property is being called into question. The mystique of the deed of ownership is melting away. In other parts of the world, peasants rise up and expropriate the land from the former owners. Blacks in America see that the deed is not eternal, that it is not signed by God, and that new deeds, making blacks the owners, can be drawn up.

The Black Muslims raised the cry, "WE MUST HAVE SOME LAND!" "SOME LAND OF OUR OWN OR ELSE!" Blacks in America shrink from the colossus of General Motors. They can't see how to wade through that thicket of common stocks, preferred stocks, bonds and debentures. They only know that General Motors is huge, that it has billions of dollars under its control, that it owns land, that its subsidiaries are legion, that it is a repository of vast powers. The blacks want to crack the nut of General Motors. They are meditating on it. Meanwhile, they must learn that the police take orders from General Motors. And that the Bank of America has something to do with them even though they don't have a righteous penny in the bank. They have no bank accounts, only bills to pay. The only way they know of making withdrawals from the bank is at the point of a gun. The shiny fronts of skyscrapers intimidate them. They do not own them. They feel alienated from the very sidewalks on which they walk. This white man's country, this white man's world. Overflowing with men of color. An economy consecrated to the succor of the whites. Blacks are incidental. The war on poverty, that monstrous insult to the rippling muscles in a black man's arms, is an index of how men actually sit down and plot each other's deaths, actually sit down with slide rules and calculate how to hide bread from the hungry. And the black bourgeoisie greedily sopping up what crumbs are tossed into their dark corner.

There are 20,000,000 of these blacks in America, probably more. Today they repeat, in awe, this magic number to themselves: there are 20,000,000 of us! They shout this to each other in humiliated astonishment. No one need tell them that there is vast power latent in their mass. They know that 20,000,000 of anything is enough to get some recognition and consideration. They know also that they must harness their number and hone it into a sword with a sharp cutting edge. White General Motors also knows that the unity of these 20,000,000 ragamuffins will spell the death of the system of its being. At all costs, then, they will seek to keep these blacks from uniting, from becoming bold and revolutionary. These white property owners know that they must keep the blacks cowardly and intimidated. By a complex communications system of hints and signals, certain orders are given to the chief of police and the sheriff, who pass them on to their men, the footsoldiers in the trenches of the ghetto.

We experience this system of control as madness. So that Leonard Deadwyler, one of these 20,000,000 blacks, is rushing his pregnant wife to the hospital and is shot dead by a policeman. An accident. That the sun rises in the east and sets in the west is also an accident, by design. The blacks are up in arms. From one end of America to the other, blacks are outraged at this accident, this latest evidence of what an accident-prone people they are, of the cruelty and pain of their lives, these blacks at the mercy of trigger-happy Yankees and Rebs in coalition against their skin. They want the policeman's blood as a sign that the Viet Cong is not the only answer. A sign to save them from the deaths they must die, and inflict. The power structure, without so much as blinking an eye, wouldn't mind tossing Bova to the mob, to restore law and order, but it knows in the vaults of its strength that at all cost the blacks must be kept at bay, that it must uphold the police department, its Guardian. Nothing must be allowed to threaten the set-up. Justice is secondary. Security is the byword.

Meanwhile, blacks are looking on and asking tactical questions. They are asked to die for the System in Vietnam. In Watts they are killed by it. Now—NOW!—they are asking each other, in dead earnest: Why not die right here in Babylon fighting for a better life, like the Viet Cong? If those little cats can do it, what's wrong with big studs like us?

A mood sets in, spreads across America, across the face of Babylon, jells in black hearts everywhere.

RACISM IN PRISON

GEORGE JACKSON

Dear Fay,[1]

On the occasion of your and Senator Dymally's tour and investigation into the affairs here at Soledad, I detected in the questions posed by your team a desire to isolate some rationale that would explain why racism exists at the prison with "particular prominence." Of course the subject was really too large to be dealt with in one tour and in the short time they allowed you, but it was a brave scene. My small but mighty mouthpiece, and the black establishment senator and his team, invading the state's maximum security row in the worst of its concentration camps. I think you are the first woman to be allowed to inspect these facilities. Thanks from all. The question was too large, however. It's tied into the question of why all these California prisons vary in character and flavor in general. It's tied into the larger question of why racism exists in this whole society with "particular prominence," tied into history. Out of it comes another question: Why do California joints produce more Bunchy Carters and Eldridge Cleavers than those over the rest of the country?

I understand [that] your attempt to isolate the set of localized circumstances that give to this particular prison's problems of race is based on a desire to aid us right now, in the present crisis. There are some changes that could be made right now that would alleviate some of the pressures inside this and other prisons. But to get at the causes, you know, one would be forced to deal with questions at the very center of Amerikan political and economic life, at the core of the Amerikan historical experience. This prison didn't come to exist where it does just by happenstance. Those who inhabit it and feed off its existence are historical products. The great majority of Soledad pigs are southern migrants who do not want to work in the fields and farms of the area, who couldn't sell cars or insurance, and who couldn't tolerate the discipline of the army. And of course prisons attract sadists. After one concedes that racism is stamped unalterably into the present nature of Amerikan sociopolitical and economic life in general

From *Soledad Brothers: The Prison Letters of George Jackson*, pp. 22–33. Published by Coward, McCann & Geoghegan, Inc., and Bantam Books, Inc.

[1] Mrs. Fay Stender, the author's lawyer.

(the definition of fascism is: a police state wherein the political ascendancy is tied into and protects the interests of the upper class—characterized by militarism, *racism,* and imperialism), and concedes further that criminals and crime arise from material, economic, sociopolitical causes, we can then burn *all* of the criminology and penology libraries and direct our attention where it will do some good.

The logical place to begin any investigation into the problems of California prisons is with our "pigs are beautiful" governor Reagan, radical reformer turned reactionary. For a real understanding of the failure of prison policies, it is senseless to continue to study the criminal. All of those who can afford to be honest know that the real victim, that poor, uneducated, disorganized man who finds himself a convicted criminal, is simply the end result of a long chain of corruption and mismanagement that starts with people like Reagan and his political appointees in Sacramento. After one investigates Reagan's character (what makes a turncoat) the next logical step in the inquiry would be a look into the biggest political prize of the state—the directorship of the Department of Corrections.

All other lines of inquiry would be like walking backward. You'll never see where you're going. You must begin with directors, assistant directors, adult authority boards, roving boards, supervisors, wardens, captains, and guards. You have to examine these people from director down to guard before you can logically examine their product. Add to this some concrete and steel, barbed wire, rifles, pistols, clubs, the tear gas that killed Brother Billingslea in San Quentin in February 1970 while he was locked in his cell, and the pick handles of Folsom, Sam Quentin, and Soledad.

To determine how men will behave once they enter the prison it is of first importance to know that prison. Men are brutalized by their environment—not the reverse.

I gave you a good example of this when I saw you last. Where I am presently being held, they never allow us to leave our cell without first handcuffing us and belting or chaining the cuffs to our waists. This is preceded always by a very thorough skin search. A force of a dozen or more pigs can be expected to invade the row at any time searching and destroying personal effects. The attitude of the staff toward the convicts is both defensive and hostile. Until the convict gives in completely it will continue to be so. By giving in, I mean prostrating oneself at their feet. Only then does their attitude alter itself to one of paternalistic condescension. Most convicts don't dig this kind of relationship (though there are some who do love it) with a group of individuals demonstrably inferior to the rest of the society in regard to education, culture, and sensitivity. Our cells are so far from the regular dining area that our food is always cold before we get it. Some days there is only one meal that can be called cooked. We *never* get anything but cold-cut sandwiches for lunch. There is no variety to the menu. The same things week after week. One is confined to his cell 23½ hours a day. Overt racism exists unchecked. It is not a case of the pigs trying to stop the many racist attacks; they actively encourage them.

They are fighting upstairs right now. It's 11:10 A.M., June 11. No black is supposed to be on the tier upstairs with anyone but other blacks but—mistakes take place—and one or two blacks end up on the tier with nine or ten white convicts frustrated by the living conditions or openly working with the pigs. The whole ceiling is trembling. In hand-to-hand combat we always win; we lose sometimes if the pigs give them knives or zip guns. Lunch will be delayed today, the tear gas or whatever it is drifts down to sting my nose and eyes. Someone is hurt bad. I hear the meat wagon from the hospital being brought up. Pigs probably gave them some weapons. But I must be fair. Sometimes (not more often than necessary) they'll set up one of the Mexican or white convicts. He'll be one who has not been sufficiently racist in his attitudes. After the brothers (enraged by previous attacks) kick on this white convict whom the officials have set up, he'll fall right into line with the rest.

I was saying that the great majority of the people who live in this area of the state and seek their employment from this institution have overt racism as a *traditional* aspect of their characters. The only stops that regulate how far they will carry this thing come from the fear of losing employment here as a result of the outside pressures to control the violence. That is O Wing, Max (Maximum Security) Row, Soledad—in part anyway.

Take an individual who has been in the general prison population for a time. Picture him as an average convict with the average twelve-year-old mentality, the nation's norm. He wants out, he wants a woman and a beer. Let's say this average convict is white and has just been caught attempting to escape. They may put him on Max Row. This is the worst thing that will ever happen to him. In the general population facility there are no chains and cuffs. TVs, radios, record players, civilian sweaters, keys to his own cell for daytime use, serve to keep his mind off his real problems. There is also a recreation yard with all sorts of balls and instruments to strike or thrust at. There is a gym. There are movies and a library well stocked with light fiction. And of course there is work, where for two or three cents an hour convicts here at Soledad make paper products, furniture, and clothing. Some people actually like this work since it does provide some money for the small things and helps them to get through their day—*without thinking* about their real problems.

Take an innocent con out of this general population setting (because a pig "thought" he may have seen him attempting a lock). Bring him to any part of O Wing (the worst part of the adjustment center of which Max Row is a part). He will be cuffed, chained, belted, pressured by the police who think that every convict should be an informer. He will be pressured by the white cons to join their racist brand of politics (they *all* go under the nickname "Hitler's Helpers"). If he is predisposed to help blacks he will be pushed away—by blacks. Three weeks is enough. The strongest hold out no more than a couple of weeks. There has been *one* white man only to go through this O Wing experience without losing his balance, without allowing himself to succumb to the madness of ribald, protrusive racism.

It destroys the logical processes of the mind, a man's thoughts become completely disorganized. The noise, madness streaming from every throat, frustrated sounds from the bars, metallic sounds from the walls, the steel trays, the iron beds bolted to the wall, the hollow sounds from a cast-iron sink or toilet.

Ironic, because one cannot get a parole to the outside prison directly from O Wing, Max Row. It's positively not done. The parole board won't even consider the Max Row case. So a man licks at the feet of the pig not for a release to the outside world but for the privilege of going upstairs to O Wing adjustment center. There the licking process must continue if a parole is the object. You can count on one hand the number of people who have been paroled to the streets from O Wing proper in all the years that the prison has existed. No one goes from O Wing, Max Row straight to the general prison population. To go from here to the outside world is unthinkable. A man *must* go from Max Row to the regular adjustment center facility upstairs. Then from there to the general prison population. Only then can he entertain thoughts of eventual release to the outside world.

One can understand the depression felt by an inmate on Max Row. He's fallen as far as he can into the social trap, relief is so distant that it is very easy for him to lose his holds. In two weeks that little average man who may have ended up on Max Row for *suspicion* of *attempted* escape is so brutalized, so completely without holds, that he will never heal again. It's worse than Vietnam.

He's dodging lead. He may be forced to fight a duel to the death with knives. If he doesn't sound and act more zealous than everyone else he will be challenged for not being loyal to his race and its politics, fascism. Some of these cons support the pigs' racism without shame, the others support it inadvertently by their own racism. The former are white, the latter black. But in here as on the street black racism is a forced *reaction.* A survival adaptation.

The picture that I have painted of Soledad's general population facility may have made it sound not too bad at all. That mistaken impression would result from the absence in my description of one more very important feature of the main line—terrorism. A frightening, petrifying diffusion of violence and intimidation is emitted from the offices of the warden and captain. How else could a small group of armed men be expected to hold and rule another much larger group except through *fear*?

We have a gym (inducement to throw away our energies with a ball instead of revolution). But if you walk into this gym with a cigarette burning, you're probably in trouble. There is a pig waiting to trap you. There's a sign "No Smoking." If you miss the sign, trouble. If you drop the cigarette to comply, trouble. The floor is regarded as something of a fire hazard (I'm not certain what the pretext is). There are no receptacles. The pig will pounce. You'll be told in no uncertain terms to scrape the cigarette from the floor with your hands. It builds from there. You have a gym but only certain things may be done and in specified ways. Since the rules change with the pigs' mood, it is really safer for a man to stay in his cell.

You have to work with emoluments that range from nothing to three cents an hour! But once you accept the pay job in the prison's industrial sector you cannot get out without going through the bad conduct process. When workers are needed, it isn't a case of accepting a job in this area. You take the job or you're automatically refusing to work, even if you clearly stated that you would cooperate in other employment. The same atmosphere prevails on the recreation yard where any type of minor mistake could result not in merely a bad conduct report and placement in adjustment center, but death. A fistfight, a temporary, trivial loss of temper will bring a fusillade of bullets down on the darker of the two men fighting.

You can't begin to measure the bad feeling caused by the existence of one TV set shared by 140 men. Think! One TV, 140 men. If there is more than one channel, what's going to occur? In Soledad's TV rooms there has been murder, mayhem, and destruction of many TV sets.

The blacks occupy one side of the room and the whites and Mexicans the other. (Isn't it significant in some way that our numbers in prison are sufficient to justify the claiming of half of all these facilities?)

We have a side, they have a side. What does your imagination envisage out of a hypothetical situation where Nina Simone sings, Angela Davis speaks, and Jim Brown "splits" on one channel, while Merle Haggard yodels and begs for an ass kicking on another. The fight will follow immediately after some brother, who is less democratic than he is starved for beauty (we did vote, but they're sixty to our forty), turns the station to see Angela Davis. What lines do you think the fighting will be along? Won't it be Angela and me against Merle Haggard?

But this situation is tolerable at least up to a point. It was worse. When I entered the joint on this offense, they had half and we had half, but our half was in the back.

In a case like the one just mentioned, the white convicts will start passing the word among themselves that all whites should be in the TV room to vote in the "Cadillac cowboy." The two groups polarize out of a situation created by whom? It's just like the outside. Nothing at all complicated about it. When people walk on each other, when disharmony is the norm, when organisms start falling apart it is the fault of those whose responsibility it is to govern. They're doing something wrong. They shouldn't have been trusted with the responsibility. And long-range political activity isn't going to help that man who will die tomorrow or tonight. The apologists recognize that these places are controlled by absolute terror, but they justify the pig's excesses with the argument that we exist outside the practice of any civilized codes of conduct. Since we are convicts rather than men, a bullet through the heart, summary execution for fistfighting or stepping across a line is not extreme or unsound at all. An official is allowed full range in violent means because a convict can be handled no other way.

Fay, have you ever considered what type of man is capable of handling absolute power. I mean how many would not abuse it? Is there any way of isolating or classifying generally who can be trusted with a gun and *absolute* discretion as to who he will kill? I've already mentioned that most of them are KKK types. The rest, all the rest, in general, are so stupid that they shouldn't be allowed to run their own bath. A *responsible* state government would have found a means of weeding out most of the savage types that are drawn to gunslinger jobs long ago. How did all these pigs get through? Men who can barely read, write, or reason. How did they get through!!? You may as well give a baboon a gun and set him loose on us!! It's the same in here as on the streets out there. *Who* has loosed this thing on an already suffering people? The Reagans, Nixons, the men who have, who own. Investigate them!! There are no qualifications asked, no experience necessary. Any fool who falls in here and can sign his name might shoot me tomorrow from a position thirty feet above my head with an automatic military rifle!! He could be dead drunk. It could really be an accident (a million to one it won't be, however), but he'll be protected still. He won't even miss a day's wages.

The textbooks on criminology like to advance the idea that prisoners are mentally defective. There is only the merest suggestion that the system itself is at fault. Penologists regard prisons as asylums. Most policy is formulated in a bureau that operates under the heading Department of Corrections. But what can we say about these asylums since *none* of the inmates are ever cured. Since in every instance they are sent out of the prison more damaged physically and mentally than when they entered. Because that is the reality. Do you continue to investigate the inmate? Where does administrative responsibility begin? Perhaps the administration of the prison cannot be held accountable for every individual act of their charges, but when things fly apart along racial lines, when the breakdown can be traced so clearly to circumstances even beyond the control of the guards and administration, investigation of anything outside the tenets of the fascist system itself is futile.

Nothing has improved, nothing has changed in the weeks since your team was here. We're on the same course, the blacks are fast losing the last of their restraints. Growing numbers of blacks are openly passed over when paroles are considered. They have become aware that their only hope lies in resistance. They have learned that resistance is actually possible. The holds are beginning to slip away. Very few men imprisoned for economic crimes or even crimes of passion against the oppressor feel that they are really guilty. Most of today's black convicts have come to understand that they are the most abused victims of an unrighteous order. Up until now, the prospect of parole has kept us from confronting our captors with any real determination.

But now with the living conditions deteriorating, and with the sure knowledge that we are slated for destruction, we have been transformed into an implacable army of liberation. The shift to the revolutionary antiestablishment position that Huey Newton, Eldridge Cleaver, and Bobby Seale projected as a solution to the problems of Amerika's black colonies has taken firm hold of these brothers' minds. They are now showing great interest in the thoughts of Mao Tse-tung, Nkrumah, Lenin, Marx, and the achievements of men like Che Guevara, Giap, and Uncle Ho.

Some people are going to get killed out of this situation that is growing. That is not a warning (or wishful thinking). I see it as an "unavoidable consequence" of placing and leaving control of our lives in the hands of men like Reagan.

These prisons have always borne a certain resemblance to Dachau and Buchenwald, places for the bad niggers, Mexicans, and poor whites. But the last ten years have brought an increase in the percentage of blacks for crimes that can *clearly* be traced to political-economic causes. There are still some blacks here who consider themselves criminals—but not many. Believe me, my friend, with the time and incentive that these brothers have to read, study, and think, you will find no class or category more aware, more embittered, desperate, or dedicated to the ultimate remedy—revolution. The most dedicated, the best of our kind—you'll find them in the Folsoms, San Quentins, and Soledads. They live like there was no tomorrow. And for most of them there isn't. Somewhere along the line they sensed this. Life on the installment plan, three years of prison, three months on parole; then back to start all over again, sometimes in the same cell. Parole officers have sent brothers back to the joint for selling newspapers (the Black Panther paper). Their official reason is "Failure to Maintain Gainful Employment," etc.

We're something like 40 to 42 percent of the prison population. Perhaps more, since I'm relying on material published by the media. The leadership of the black prison population now definitely identifies with Huey, Bobby, Angela, Eldridge, and antifascism. The savage repression of blacks, which can be estimated by reading the obituary columns of the nation's dailies, Fred Hampton, etc., has not failed to register on the black inmates. The holds are fast being broken. Men who read Lenin, Fanon, and Che don't riot, "they mass," "they rage," they dig graves.

When John Clutchette was first accused of this murder he was proud, conscious, aware of his own worth but uncommitted to any specific remedial action. Review the process that they are sending this beautiful brother through now. It comes at the end of a long train of similar incidents in his prison life. Add to this all of the things he has witnessed happening to others of our group here. Comrade Fleeta spent eleven months here in O Wing for possessing photography taken from a newsweekly. It is such things that explain why California prisons produce more than their share of Bunchy Carters and Eldridge Cleavers.

Fay, there are only two types of blacks ever released from these places, the Carters and the broken men.

The broken men are so damaged that they will never again be suitable members of any sort of social unit. Everything that was still good when they entered the joint, anything inside of them that may have escaped the ruinous effects of black colonial existence, anything that may have been redeemable when they first entered the joint—is gone when they leave.

This camp brings out the very best in brothers or destroys them entirely. But none are unaffected. None who leave here are normal. If I leave here alive, I'll leave nothing behind. They'll never count me among the broken men, but I can't say that I am normal either. I've been hungry too long. I've gotten angry too often. I've been lied to and insulted too many times. They've pushed me over the line from which there can be no retreat. I *know* that they will not be satisfied until they've pushed me out of this existence altogether. I've been the victim of so many racist attacks that I could never relax again. My reflexes will never be normal again. I'm like a dog that has gone through the K-9 process.

This is not the first attempt the institution (camp) has made to murder me. It is the most determined attempt, but not the first.

I look into myself at the close of every one of these pretrial days for any changes that may have taken place. I can still smile now, after ten years of blocking knife thrusts and pick handles of faceless sadistic pigs, of anticipating and reacting for ten years, seven of them in solitary. I can still smile sometimes, but by the time this thing is over I may not be a nice person. And I just lit my seventy-seventh cigarette of this twenty-one-hour day. I'm going to lay down for two or three hours, perhaps I'll sleep . . .

Seize the Time.

FOUR

Controlling the Dangerous Classes: Punishment and Social Structure

> . . . it is necessary to strip from the social institution of punishment its ideological veils and juristic appearance and to describe it in its real relationships.
>
> **Rusche and Kirchheimer, 1968:5**

Prison writers and the larger prison movement argue that the function of the contemporary penal system is to maintain privilege. A history of the growth and transition of punishment and correction offers the clearest possible linkage between privilege and the manner in which societies suppress classes of individuals who are considered threats to the existing social structure. In the literature on penology one work stands alone in demonstrating the relationship between crime and privilege more than any other research in criminology: *Punishment and Social Structure*, by George Rushe and Otto Kirchheimer (first published in 1939). In this chapter we will present a distillation of their ideas and briefly summarize the historical development of penal practice in Europe and the United States.

In his introduction to a 1968 edition of Rusche and Kirchheimer's study, Thorsten Sellin states that the idea that "punishment" and "protection of society" are conflicting goals is historically incorrect. Sellin argues that all punishment or penal treatment is aimed at protecting society. But *Society* must be thought of in terms of systems of

This chapter is based upon Rusche and Kirchheimer's classic history of punishment, *Punishment and Social Structure* (1968).

privilege and different levels of power. Sellin concludes that "the aim of all punishment is the protection of those social values which the dominant social group of a state regard as good for society" (Sellin, in Rusche and Kirchheimer, 1968: vi). The techniques employed by the state are those believed to be the best to secure obedience. Sellin explains that the selection of the "best" correctional techniques is a function of a society's traditions, its level of knowledge, and its economic and social conditions. This insight into the bonds between social relations and penal systems is very often lacking in standard histories of punishment; these traditional works spend a good deal of time discussing abstract theories of the purposes of punishment or providing historical descriptions without attempting to connect personal troubles to public issues.

Rusche and Kirchheimer criticize traditional studies of penology because they believe these are restricted by the need to defend the ideological integrity of punishment. They argue, further, that the history of punishment is presented as the "unfolding of an idea": penological developments are bound together with the ideological notions of "progress" and "reform." A more sophisticated understanding of the history of punishment requires that one consider penal changes in relation to changes in social structure.

> Punishment is neither a simple consequence of crime, nor the reverse side of crime, nor a mere means which is determined by the end to be achieved. . . . The transformation in penal systems cannot be explained only from changing needs of the war against crime, although this struggle does play a part. Every system of production tends to discover punishments which correspond to its productive relationships. It is thus necessary to investigate the origin and fate of penal systems, the use or avoidance of specific punishments, and the intensity of penal practices as they are determined by social forces, above all by economic and then fiscal forces. (Rusche and Kirchheimer, 1968:5)

Rusche and Kirchheimer accomplish this task by examining the forms of punishment in particular historical periods; social, economic, and political changes; and the related development of penal ideologies.

Penal systems are designed to control those classes of individuals who pose a threat to the status quo. Rusche and Kirchheimer assert that if we consider the actual structure of modern society, the principal targets of punishment are the underprivileged social strata: "Penalties must be of such a nature that the latter will fear a further decline in their mode of existence." (*Ibid.*, p. 6) The specific form of punishment corresponds to a specific stage of economic development: enslavement as a penalty requires a slave economy; prison labor is impossible without manufacture and industry; and a system of monetary fines for all classes of society requires a money economy. When a given productive system disappears, the corresponding punishments become inapplicable. New developments in the economic order must be introduced into the social structure before new penal systems can be incorporated into the social and economic system. The house of correction, precursor of the modern prison, reached its peak during the age of mercantilism and was intimately related to the development of this mode of production. The use of industrial capitalism and the factory system decreased the economic importance of the sixteenth-century houses of correction and, in turn, produced new forms of penal practice. The transition to modern industrial society brought with it a free-labor system, and this minimized the economic role of convict labor. As inmate labor became less and less important in production, the choice of penal methods derived largely from *fiscal* considerations. Punishment systems in modern industrial societies depend heavily upon the financial prerequisites of the state. Specifically, this has meant attempts to decrease the costs of punishments, but this tendency is tempered by the necessity of the State to maintain order and to control challenges to the privilege structure.[1]

The history of penal methods can be divided into several epochs, in which entirely different systems prevailed. Penance and fines were dominant methods of punishment in the early Middle Ages. The later Middle Ages witnessed the rise of a cruel system of corporal and capital punishment, which was replaced during the seventeenth century by imprisonment as the major mode of punishment. The modern period is characterized by an intricate system of imprisonment, fines, and supervised release systems such as probation and parole. This chapter will be devoted to a sketch of the changes in social structure that accompanied various penal "reforms" in these epochs.

Penance and Fines

The early Middle Ages did not exhibit an elaborate system of state

[1] The declining tax revenues and increasing expenditures of the state has been analyzed by James O'Connor in *The Fiscal Crisis of the State* (1973).

punishment. Legal systems essentially governed relations among equals in status and wealth. The economic bases of the legal system assumed the existence of sufficient land to accommodate an increasing population without lowering their standard of living. The colonization of Eastern Europe produced a constant demand for labor, which enabled the agricultural population to escape pressures by landlords on their serfs to produce foodstuffs and other products. The growth of new towns in the thirteenth century allowed serfs to escape and attain their freedom. These economic facts prodded the landowners to treat their serfs with more care. Relations between the warrior-landlords and their serfs were governed by traditions that were equivalent to precisely defined legal relationships. The traditional social structure of the early Middle Ages tended to promote social cohesion and prevent social tensions. A well-balanced system of social dependence supported by religious conceptions that legitimated the established social order made formal criminal law unimportant as a means of preserving the social hierarchy.

Criminal law focused upon the maintenance of public order among social equals. The legal system of the era was a private arbitration system relying almost completely upon the imposition of fines. If an individual committed an offense against the prevailing codes of decency, morality, or religion, a body of free men would convene and make the offender pay *Wergeld* (a fine) or do penance so that individual disputes would not escalate into blood feuds or open warfare. Crime was considered an act of war, and in the absence of a strong centralized state the public peace was quite fragile—endangered by the smallest quarrels.

Differences in privilege were expressed in the extent of penance demanded by various social offenders: the system of penance was graded according to the social status of the offender and of the victim. Initially, class distinctions manifested themselves in punishment only in the degree of penance required, but soon the privileged evolved a system of corporal punishment: "The inability of lower-class evildoers to pay fines in money led to the substitution of corporal punishment in their case. The penal system thus came to be more and more restricted to a minority of the population." (*Ibid.*, p. 9) During this time prisons were used primarily to hold offenders who were to receive corporal punishment in lieu of payment of fines.

Early medieval private law was transformed into an instrument of domination. Feudal lords used their own penal codes to discipline those who were economically disadvantaged. The only limit upon the lord's disciplinary power was a jurisdictional claim by another lord. During this period the system of private criminal law declined because of the struggles of central authorities such as kings and princes to consolidate their power. Moreover, fines provided a valuable source of income to the ruling elites. Fines and the costs of legal proceedings produced revenue that sometimes included the offender's confiscated property. Rusche and Kirchheimer believe that the attempt to extract revenue as part of the administration of justice was one of the principal factors in transforming the private system of arbitration into the public system of centralized authority.

Social-Structure Change during the Middle Ages

The plight of the lower classes deteriorated throughout most of Europe during the fifteenth century. European population began to rise after the plagues of the fourteenth century, and the urban population increased rapidly. "The number of the downtrodden, unemployed, and propertyless people rose everywhere" (*Ibid.*, p. 11). The rising population density in certain areas as well as primitive means of cultivation led to the exhaustion of much fertile land. The rise of the urban populace generated a demand for cheap grain. Whereas landowners had previously permitted small farmers to rent land for nominal fees, the few markets made agricultural production extremely profitable and drove up the value of land.

Increasing birth rates together with the restriction of free spaces on the land gradually created a reserve labor pool, which allowed landlords to depress the living standards of the peasantry. By the beginning of the sixteenth century, the oppression of the agricultural labor force had reached unheard-of extremes. The shift from agriculture to grazing and the development of a capitalistic pasturage system further contributed to the pauperization of the lower classes. Dissatisfied peasants streamed into medieval towns.[2]

The workers and artisans of the towns were threatened by the mass immigration of the impoverished peasantry. Everywhere, production did not keep pace with population increase. Various municipalities imposed restrictions (Poor Laws) upon the new migrants—preventing them from obtaining citizenship, preventing them from joining the guilds, and even closing the gates of the cities to them. The displaced

[2] Recall the case of the French town of Lyons, discussed in Chapter Two.

agricultural population were forced to remain on the roads; many resorted to begging or banding together in vagabondage. The medieval world had yet to develop a coherent policy with which to deal with the growth of the "dangerous class." The migrants were recruited as mercenary troops by ambitious princes who found them a cheap source of soldiers with which they could consolidate and extend their power. The peasant-soldiers made knights superfluous and cost them most of their income. Many of the knights, privileged by birth but landless, took to highway robbery, and the under classes did the same on a smaller scale. The destitute peasants robbed openly, whereas the knights justified their crimes under the pretext of warfare or the demands of chivalry. There were attempts to lower the birth rate by prohibiting marriages, but this resulted in a rise in the number of illegitimate children.

The exploitation of the pauperized masses led to the accumulation of huge fortunes. The entrepreneurs of the towns had an abundant, cheap pool of labor to apply to their economic pursuits. Capitalists began to assert their economic strength and lengthened the distance between those who could extend credit and capital and those who were wage laborers. Many researchers of this period record a dramatic drop in wages paid to workers. Declining wages led to strikes and boycotts and, in turn, retaliation by masters. Violence resulting from war, class struggle, and criminality was accompanied by the rise of scarcity and misery.

The Rise of Capitalism and the Growth of Criminal Law

Intense forms of class struggle in fourteenth- and fifteenth-century Europe led to the growth of a harsh criminal law system directed against the lower classes. The ruling class sought methods to make the administration of justice more effective in slowing the rise in crime, especially in the big towns. The system of fines and corporal punishment continued, but class distinctions became increasingly significant in the application of justice. The private settlement of disputes declined, particularly in cases where there was evidence of "dishonesty." Gradually, the imputation of "dishonesty" came to be applied regularly to the lower-class offender. For example, the term "villain," which originally designated a member of a particular social class, came to denote moral inferiority. Upper-class offenders were generally treated more leniently in criminal cases.

The growing urban bourgeoisie became especially occupied with the rise in criminality. They used their influence in legislative bodies to secure new crime control methods. Initially, they appealed for more efficiency in the criminal justice system and more repressive punishments. This historical period saw the introduction of vagrancy laws based primarily on the offender's "honesty"—a term that, as we have noted, had clear social-class implications.[3] Criminal justice continued to be an instrument of privilege: the wealthy bought exemptions from punishments and the poor were powerless to protect themselves from harsh treatment. The immense poverty of the period created an army of vagabonds, beggars, and robbers, which was seen as a real threat to social stability. As the impoverishment of the masses continued, punishments grew harsher and more brutal. Physical punishment increased in frequency until it became the primary form of penal treatment. "Execution, mutilation, and flogging were not introduced at one stroke by any sudden revolutionary change, but gradually became the rule with changing conditions." (*Ibid.,* p. 18) Harsh punishments continued.

Before the fifteenth century, capital punishment and mutilation of offenders were used only in extreme cases and only to supplement the system of penance and fines, but in time these became the most common penal measures. Judges used these penal remedies in cases in which they believed the offender to be a "threat to society." The sixteenth century witnessed an extraordinary increase in the application of the death penalty. Rusche and Kirchheimer report that 72,000 thieves were hanged during the reign of Henry VIII and that under Elizabeth vagabonds were strung up in rows, "as many as three or four hundred at a time." (The citizenry of England at this time numbered only about three million.) The application of the death penalty was altered in principle. No longer simply the extreme penalty for serious offenders, the death penalty became a method of disposing of large numbers of allegedly dangerous persons. Historians of the period tell us that little attention was paid to the guilt or innocence of the suspect. Torture was often used to coerce confessions from alleged offenders as well as to gather information about possible accomplices.

Methods of execution became more brutal. The public debated how to devise more painful means of imposing the death penalty. Mutilating offenders permanently labeled them as criminals; often the victims of penal mutilation died as a result of the process. Exile as a

[3] See William Chamblis on the social function of vagrancy laws (1973).

means of punishment during this age had different impacts upon members of different social classes. For the privileged, exile might mean travel for study, new business relations, or even diplomatic service—with the prospect of an early and honorable return. For the poor, exile might mean escape from death in their own town; but, often, poor offenders faced death penalties in the places where they sought refuge.

The system of punishment in the later Middle Ages made it clear that there was no labor shortage, particularly in the towns. Wages declined and the value placed upon human life by the ruling classes decreased. The system of punishment intensified the struggle for existence among the poor. Criminologist Hans von Hentig argued that the function of this type of penal system was to destroy those whom the ruling elite considered unfit for society.[4] Much has been written about the participation of the masses in the public executions of the era. But this participation should be interpreted in the light of social conditions. The people of the Middle Ages lived in conditions of oppression, hatred, and desperation. Their seeming inability to affect world affairs led many to express their fury and sorrow in supernatural or quasi-religious terms. Superstition was widespread; witches were pursued and blamed for the misfortunes of the masses. Public executions were steeped in bizarre ritual, and popular sentiment held that mutilation and death penalties could appease supernatural forces. The persecution of witches, Jews, and outlaws represented a social expression of bad times and a supposed solution to personal problems. The widely reported sadism and savagery of the medieval masses should be understood in light of their social and economic oppression. Rather than serving as a deterrent to crime, public executions suited the impoverishment of the lower classes.

The penal system of the later Middle Ages did not slow the increase in crime. But neither was it a mere reflection of human irrationality: "Brutal punishments cannot be ascribed simply to the primitive cruelty of an epoch now vanished. Cruelty itself is a social phenomenon which can be understood only in terms of the social relationships prevailing in any given period." (*Ibid.*, p. 23)

The Rise of Imprisonment

By the end of the sixteenth century methods of punishment had undergone a significant but gradual change. The possibility of

[4] See von Hentig's *Punishment: Its Origin, Purpose and Psychology* (1937).

exploiting the labor of prisoners gained greater acceptance. Galley slavery, deportation, and penal servitude were introduced, first to supplement existing systems of punishment but later as replacements. These penal reforms were not motivated primarily by humanitarian concerns; they were promoted by changes in the social structure that enhanced the potential value of the human material that was completely at the disposal of the State.

Larger and wealthier towns increased their demand for consumer goods. The growth of the financial system led to a constant expansion of markets. Trade relations established in the Mediterranean region and in Asia produced new sources of wealth. The conquest of territories increased the importation of precious metals and extended the market for exported goods. At the same time, the European population began to decline because of religious wars and civil strife. Some estimate this decline at from 30 to 50 percent during the first half of the seventeenth century.

The combination of a declining labor pool and a growing economy produced a rise in wages. Both agricultural and crafts workers became scarce, and this resulted in more favorable wage scales and working conditions. Ironically, the poor laws enacted during the earlier period prevented the free movement of laborers from town to town. These laws forced the poor to remain in their native towns and thus prevented a rational distribution of labor. Abject poverty and unemployment in one town coincided with labor scarcity in another. The propertied classes were faced with the prospect of paying high wages to attract the scarce labor supply, an economic situation that contrasted sharply with that of the previous century. The accumulation of capital necessary for the expansion of trade and manufacture was limited by new wage and working conditions. Faced with an extremely undesirable labor situation, the capitalist classes appealed to the state to remedy their financial plight.

The solution most apparent to the ruling class was to increase the birth rate. Politicians, clergymen, and economists argued for measures to increase marriages and the number of children. Tax incentives were offered for early marriages and large families. Laws prohibited the clergy from sanctioning unwed mothers, and the customary one-year period of mourning for widows was condemned. Attempts were made to stop infanticide.

Armies were depleted because of the increasingly favorable working conditions. These manpower shortages led to the use of criminals in military service.

> Judges and gaolers were consulted about the fitness of convicts for military service and the qualification was physical, not moral. The army came to be considered a kind of penal organization suited only for ne'er-do-wells, spendthrifts, black sheep, and ex-convicts. (*Ibid.*, p. 30)

Countries took criminals from other governments that had no military use for them. Criminals sometimes perceived military service as a practical means of avoiding prosecution.

The state was clearly aligned with the interests of capital. Migration of labor was strictly forbidden, governments supplied credit to manufacturers, and rights were granted to "royal monopolies." States imposed maximum wage scales to halt the rise in wages due to the free competition of labor. Prevailing economic theory held that a country could become rich only if there was a large pool of poor people forced to work to avoid abject poverty. It was believed that the incentive to work would be destroyed if the living conditions of the masses were vastly improved.[5] Laws established working hours of between twelve and sixteen hours per day. Associations of workers were prohibited, and laborers were severely punished for work stoppages.

Child labor was widely encouraged. The state provided manufacturers with children from orphanages. Educational systems were structured to train children for industry. Theorists argued that child labor prevented children from involvement in mischief and taught them to aid their families financially. But the introduction of child labor as well as the other practices mentioned above did not seem sufficient to affect the shortage of labor, and the state thus instituted systems of forced labor.

The labor reserve of the state was composed primarily of those who had violated the law or those under state supervision, such as orphans, widows, and lunatics. Treatment of the poor and dependent can best be understood in relation to the history of charity and the development of criminal law. Careful examination of the treatment of the poor, the dependent, and the insane offers substantial support for a more general theory of social control and privilege.

Redefining the functions and methods of charity precipitated religious and social-class disputes. Catholic Church doctrine held that aiding the poor was an act of religious obligation. Those who chose voluntary poverty were viewed as performing an act of sacred

[5] One finds this same ideology dominant in contemporary debates over welfare programing and minimum-wage laws.

importance. Giving to the poor was believed to please God. The accumulated property of the Church was justified as belonging to the aged, the poor, and the sick. The rising bourgeois class held a contrary position on poverty, however. They made a sharp distinction between unworthy, able-bodied poor and legitimate paupers, emphasizing work as a necessary and desirable component of life. The bourgeoisie received its clearest support in the religious doctrines of Calvinism: "They found in Calvinism a theoretical foundation for their ascetic attitude and for their concept of the calling, an attitude toward economic problems which was a necessity for them." (*Ibid.*, p. 36) The Calvinist insistence on the necessity of work and the doctrine that those rewarded by material wealth on earth were "saved" in eternity fit perfectly with the emerging economic system and its need for an extensive, disciplined work force.

Calvinist philosophy could not justify supporting beggars who, out of "laziness," refused to work. Poor laws soon contained the justifications of this new religious doctrine of punishing the "unworthy" poor. Many Catholic towns soon regulated vagrancy and begging with laws similar to those in Protestant municipalities. The acute shortage of labor inevitably became related to the perceived "plague of the beggars." Laws broadened the definition of vagrants to include all who refused to work at prevailing wage rates. Many statutes attempted to prevent workers from withholding their labor. And by the close of the seventeenth century, the house of correction had become, in response to economic conditions, a significant part of penal policy.

The Bridewell in London (1555) is considered the first institution designed specifically to control beggars and vagrants. By 1576 an act of Parliament provided for the establishment of similar institutions in every English county. In Europe the most famous of these houses of correction was established in Amsterdam at the close of the sixteenth century.[6] Visitors from throughout Europe came to visit and study this innovation in penology. The house of correction combined the principles of the poorhouse, workhouse, and penal institution. Its main objective was to harness the labor of unwilling people. Prisoners were forced to work within the institution and would thus develop the habits of industry as well as receive vocational training. The inmates of the Amsterdam house of correction were supposed to enter the labor market upon their release.

[6] The most complete description of the Amsterdam house of correction is provided in Sellin's *Pioneering in Penology* (1944).

Typical inmates of houses of correction included beggars, vagrants, prostitutes, and petty thieves. Later, these institutions received offenders sentenced to long terms. As the reputation of these houses developed, citizens committed their delinquent children and unwanted dependents to them. Other houses of correction confined all the poor and needy. The French *Hôpitaux généraux* fed and gave work to widows and orphans. This French experiment in corrections was first begun in Paris in 1656 but was soon spread throughout France by the Jesuits.

Administrators of the houses of correction either ran the institutions themselves or hired out the laborers to private contractors. Men were used to rasp hardwoods used by the dyeing industry—an important industry in Amsterdam. Prisoners, working in pairs with a huge saw, produced three hundred pounds of wood weekly. This was difficult work requiring stamina and great strength. Eighteenth-century houses of correction introduced wool manufacture, which was more profitable. Women inmates were employed in textile production.

An official decree of the Spandau house of correction in Germany bluntly announced that the purpose of the institution was to produce textiles and to remedy the lack of spinning wheels in the countries. Contracts with lessees provided for treatment of inmates that would not render them incapable of work. To promote the economic efficiency of the houses of correction, inmates were required to continue working long after they completed their "training," in order to repay the cost of their board and education.

The guilds opposed the workhouses because the prison labor endangered their monopolies. Several lawsuits were brought by guilds to stop the whole system of houses of correction. The French *Hôpitaux* experimented with technological innovations and new labor arrangements. This often brought charges by private businessmen of unfair competition. In response, the administrators of the houses of correction allowed private entrepreneurs to use their facilities, and there is some evidence that the forced labor of prisoners was used by capitalists to gain monopolies in certain industries.

The ultimate economic value of the early houses of correction is open to question. Some authors report extraordinary profits, but others report that production was low and that administrators were often corrupt. Houses of correction represented an early example of state expenditures aiding private enterprise. Moreover, the houses of correction firmly established the idea that confinement without forced labor was no punishment: "The institution of houses of correction in such a society was not the result of brotherly love or of an official sense of obligation to the distressed. It was part of the development of capitalism." (*Ibid.*, p. 50)

These forerunners of the modern prison were symbolic supports for the work ethic and the industrial discipline necessary for the growth of capitalism. Early religious disputes over the role of the poor were substantially resolved as the Protestant houses of correction and the Catholic *Hôpitaux généraux* united under the ideology generated by the economic movement of the times.

Galley Slavery and Transportation

The relationship between the economic structure and penal practice is clear-cut in the cases of galley slavery and transportation. As the economic value of human life rose, the state found methods of using criminals' labor.

Galley slavery grew out of the need for rowers to propel sailing vessels in Mediterranean waters. Wars heightened the demand for oarsmen and this led to the drafting of prisoners into galley slavery. Each ship needed approximately 350 oarsmen, and the work was hazardous and difficult. Many European powers used galley slavery initially as the form of punishment for senior offenders, but this penal practice was soon extended to beggars and the "unworthy poor." Some rulers preferred to sentence criminals to galley slavery rather than executing them, for galley slavery rendered them service and was believed to be a higher form of penance for sins. Galley slavery is especially significant because its economic implications often triumphed over penal goals. In France, for instance, the courts were instructed by the Crown to convict criminals more quickly in order to fill the need for oarsmen. Judicial administrators in Europe in general sometimes went as far as organizing hunts for potential felons who could be sentenced to galley servitude.

Galley slavery was designed to extract the maximum amount of labor from convicts. Sentences were often for ten years so that men "could get their sea legs," at which point it would be foolish to free them because they were then most useful to the state. Some forms of galley servitude were fixed at twelve years because the labor value of convicts deteriorated after that length of time, and there appeared no good reason to clothe and feed convicts without a return in labor.

In the seventeenth century, galley slavery was thought to be more humane than prior penal methods: men who would have been sentenced to death or exiled were spared and performed productive work for the State. However, "the texts of the decrees and orders make it quite clear that the substitution of galley labor for the death penalty was a result of a need for more oarsmen and not of humanitarian considerations. They provide for commutation only on the basis of bodily strength, not special circumstances justifying clemency." (*Ibid.*, p. 57)

Many convicts mutilated themselves in an attempt to avoid being sentenced to the galleys. The practice was apparently so widespread that it was made punishable by the death penalty. Reports of galley servitude tell of brutal conditions: "Galley labor was tantamount to a slow and painful death." *(Ibid.)* In this cruel system prisoners performed tasks that free laborers would never perform, even in the worst of times. Reformation of convicts was not a consideration in the galley system, which ended only when refinements in the art of navigation eliminated the need for galley labor.

Transportation—the shipping of convicts to distant colonies—was another important use of prisoners' labor. England's vast colonial empire led to the most extensive system of transportation of criminals. Vast tracts of English colonial lands were to be formed, and laborers were needed for this. Initially, settlers attempted to enslave the native populations, but these groups resisted and were decimated by colonial wars. Natives who were enslaved often died as a result of harsh labor and disease. An alternative was to import laborers. This often led to the kidnaping of children and the poor, who were then sold into slavery in the colonies. The deportation of convicts to the colonies was a partial solution to the problem of delivering workers to the overseas territories without depleting the labor pool at home. Commutation of sentence was based upon the physical fitness of the transported prisoner, as it was with the galley slave. Between 1718 and 1720 transportation became the standard sentence for larceny and theft. Initially, colonial contractors received grants of five pounds for each inmate they accepted, but later, as they became owners of the convicts through a system of indentured servitude, they derived sufficient profit from the labor of their penal slaves. The number of convicts shipped to North America was quite large: "The Old Bailey alone supplied at least 10,000 between 1717 and 1775." (*Ibid.*, p.60)

Deported convicts were assigned to penal servitude for a fixed period of time, after which they were freed. Many of these penal laborers eventually became independent farmers and planters. In contrast, African peoples pressed into slavery were perpetually the property of their owners. The use of African slaves eventually supplanted the transportation system. African slaves were considered much more valuable because of the indeterminate length of their servitude; thus, as the African slave trade flourished, the deportation of convicts ceased to be a paying proposition. The American Revolutionary War brought the transportation system to an abrupt end.

The decline of galley slavery and transportation contributed to the use of prisons as a form of punishment. Prior to the eighteenth century, jails were places in which persons were confined until they came to trial. A secondary function of prisons was to confine persons who failed to pay fines or who were to receive corporal punishment. Jailers received their incomes from the fees collected from inmates. But the success of the house of correction during the mercantile era (the 1500s and 1600s) suggested the idea of exploiting the labor of the confined offender. Eighteenth-century jails evolved into manufacturing houses, in which the reformation of prisoners was secondary to economic motives. This is illustrated by the fact that release was dependent upon the labor value of the prisoner. Valuable workers were retained as long as possible, and their length of confinement was arbitrarily fixed by the jail administrators. The indeterminate prison sentence originated directly from the desire to efficiently exploit prisoner labor. As the inmate population continued to swell throughout Europe, penal spokesmen celebrated the concept that prisons and jails would pay for themselves and thus relieve the state of a fiscal burden: "The evolution of this unprofitable business into a system which was partially self-supporting from the standpoint of the treasury and a successful part of national industry from the standpoint of mercantilist policy paved the way for the introduction of imprisonment as a regular form of punishment." (*Ibid.*, p. 69) Those prisons used exclusively for detaining persons who were awaiting trial (and who were therefore not capable of being commercially exploited) remained in bad condition until the nineteenth century.

Prisons operated by the Catholic Church were oriented more toward the reformation of the delinquent and the maintenance of Church discipline. The French cleric Father Mabillon was one of the first writers to discuss the rehabilitative function of imprisonment. In his famous essay, "Réflexions sur les Prisons des Ordres Religieux" (1724), Mabillon argued that prisoners should work, but only for their moral redemption. Mabillon believed that charity should be the essential element of punishment and that penal sanctions should be proportionate to the gravity of the offense, as well as to the bodily and spiritual strength of the offender. He advocated a graded system of prison favors, accorded in relation to evidence of moral regeneration. Disciplinary measures and release, according to Mabillon, should be related to individual reformation. The French cleric expressed ideas quite different from the straightforward economic motives that molded the secular penal system. Later, some of Mabillon's theological precepts would be merged with labor exploitation goals to form the contours of the modern penal system.

Criminal Law and Penal Theory in the Age of Enlightenment

The Age of Enlightenment, which occurred during the eighteenth century in Europe, has been given a great deal of attention by criminologists. Conventional theories interpret the period as a crucial one in the development of a humane and just system of penal practice. Upon closer scrutiny, however, we find that the reforms of this era primarily benefited a particular segment of the privileged class and that the changes in social structure continued to shape the administration of justice and the system of punishment. Becarria wrote his classic *Essay on Crimes and Punishments* during this period, and it produced widespread political debate. Reformers of the period addressed themselves to the nature of punishment and the current status of criminal procedure.

The question of punishment was still largely a question of what to do with the lower classes. Legal concerns, however, were tied more closely to the interests of the bourgeoisie, who were struggling for political power and seeking legal guarantees for their own security. The reformers spoke for the bourgeoisie and against the unrestrained power of the aristocratic rulers. They condemned a criminal justice system that did not appear to be governed by fixed rules, a system in which judges exercised arbitary powers to fix penalties and used law enforcement techniques that failed to protcct the accused. The primary goal of reform was to limit the power of the state to punish by creating fixed rules and by enforcing rigid controls on judicial authorities. Specifically, reformers sought an exact correlation between a particular punishment and a particular crime. "Punishment must fit the crime" was the rallying cry of the day. Some, such as

Bentham, worked out precise mathematical relations between the gradations of offenses and the gradations of punishment.

Enlightenment thinkers favored a definite and predictable legal system that left no room for judicial discretion. Judicial decisions should be based solely on the facts of the case. In principle, they rejected class privileges in law. Becarria and others argued that punishments should be set at the minimum level of severity in order to prevent crime. Both Becarria and Voltaire warned that the current arbitrary and harsh system of justice could lead to social unrest: "The attenuation of punishment thus becomes a practical measure of defense against social revolution as well as against individual acts." (*Ibid.,* p. 76). The bourgeois theorists wanted to protect and defend the rights of property, and they based their criticism of the existing system on its inefficiency. Often, the reformers claimed that juries would acquit guilty persons because of the terrible punishment they might receive if convicted.

Enlightenment writers argued for harsh punishment when the social order was menaced. Otherwise, their general principle was freedom of movement and action (which better fitted the interests of the privileged than the lower classes). The rising bourgeois class wanted a criminal justice system that acted *swiftly, reliably,* and *predictably.*

Reformers focused their efforts in demands for public jury trials, free choice of a lawyer, suppression of torture, clearly defined rules of evidence, and protection against illegal imprisonment. These demands for *formal legal rationality* were put forth on behalf of all classes, but the impact of the new procedures on the various social classes differed widely: "The lower classes . . . could seldom avail themselves of the complicated trial machinery which the law set up for them as well as for the wealthy since they lacked the necessary knowledge or financial resources." (*Ibid.,* p. 78) Then, as now, the structure of privilege and the reality of social injustice invalidated the promise of formal legal justice for the under classes. The fundamental civil rights that were in principle extended to all did not stop the oppression of the poor through the harsh enforcement of vagrancy and poor laws.

Penal Practice and the Industrial Revolution

The movement towards criminal law reform advocated by Becarria and others gained political strength near the end of the eighteenth century. But at this same time the widespread need for manpower, which structured the early penal system, was disappearing. This change was first observed in the declining conditions of the houses of correction. In their heyday these institutions were clean and well managed, but contemporary observers such as John Howard reported deplorable conditions and decay. "Neglect, intimidation, and torment of inmates became the rule of the day, and they were given work only for their discomfort or for the profit to be gained." (*Ibid.,* p. 85)

The houses of correction flourished during times when labor conditions were favorable to the lower classes. This situation changed as the demand for workers was satisfied and a surplus developed. Population throughout Europe increased steadily. The ruling class began to realize its dream of relative overpopulation. Work became scarce, especially with the expansion of the factory system. The eighteenth century saw a new influx of agricultural workers into the cities—a movement that continued into the nineteenth century.

The introduction of machinery had drastic effects upon the lower classes. Textile industries were the first to develop a mechanized technology. Spinning, once a home-based industry for the poorer classes, was transformed into a factory industry that employed women and children. Unemployment rose but so did production.

The middle classes benefited from the new economic developments, but they felt hampered by the special favors that the government granted to a few. The bourgeoisie demanded freedom of trade, freedom of manufacture, and free competition. Employers wanted to end state regulation of work conditions because they felt they could do better in an unfettered competitive situation. "Laissez faire, laissez passer" was the motto of the day. Individualism and free competition was the new utopian solution. Adam Smith's "invisible hand" would somehow ensure that the social order would be maintained. Workers suffered under this new ideology because the labor market was saturated. Historians record the rapid decline in wages and the enormous misery of the working class during this time. The legal coercions needed to secure workers in the mercantile age were no longer needed and were gradually abandoned.

Economic theorists who wished to preserve the existing system of privilege, rejected an artificial increase in wages (such as a minimum wage law) because this would deplete the fund available for capital investment and lead to more unemployment. Malthus and others criticized the encouragement of population growth during the Mercantile Era and predicted that increasing birth rates would lead to widespread starvation and crime. Marriages among the poor, they argued, would fill the land with children destined to a life of vice and shame. They demanded measures to stop illegitimacy and to require government consent for marriage.

The system of poor relief broke down entirely. The *Hôpitaux* and the poorhouses were sharply criticized. Deaths from starvation rose. Malthus argued that the condition of the poor could be raised only at the expense of the remainder of the working class. Benevolence toward the poor, according to Malthus, would lead to an increase in population and thus create more misery. But Malthus and others did not advocate the abandonment of the poor because they believed that this might lead to revolution.

The working class demanded the right to work—a turn of events for the upper class, which had urgently sought labor power in an earlier age. The factory replaced the house of correction as a source of labor because the penal institution required a greater financial outlay for administration and discipline. Free labor could produce more than prison labor, and the houses of correction decayed because of this.

The intensity of the struggle for existence drove many of the impoverished to crime. Statistics for the first quarter of the nineteenth century reveal a rapid increase in property crimes. The ruling class responded with demands for a return to the harsher punishments of premercantile times. The use of imprisonment came under attack: "The axe, the whip, and starvation ought to be introduced in order to root out the criminals." (quoted in Rusche and Kirchheimer, 1968:97) Many argued for the extensive use of the death penalty and life imprisonment. It is interesting to note that the penal codes of this age increased the severity of punishment but left the procedural reforms of the Enlightenment reformers untouched. The formal rules of fixing guilt were believed to be moral support for harsh punishment of the guilty.

Imprisonment became the chief form of punishment of the age. Class privileges were still reflected in the scale of punishments, despite the arguments of the Enlightenment reformers. It was argued that the principle of equality could be abandoned in the case of minor penalties as long as this did not give immunity to serious offenders. Penal authorities argued that the upper classes were more sensitive to punishment and that there was a greater likelihood of punishment bringing hardships upon their families. Many European countries provided for separate confinement of upper-class prisoners.

Existing prisons, which were designed primarily to hold persons awaiting trial, became inadequate because of their increased population. Jails became quickly overcrowded and there was neither time nor money to build new prisons; other public buildings were pressed into service. State officials became increasingly reluctant to provide funds for prison upkeep. Several reports from this period detail the horrid unsanitary conditions that led to sickness, starvation, and, often, death. Prison populations grew immensely at a time when the economic utility of penal confinement was considered small. Critics of the prevailing conditions in jails noted the inadequate supply of food and the spread of contagious diseases, and some observed that effective punishment was not possible.

Prison reformers of this age believed that the terrible prison conditions of the early nineteenth century were attributable to corrupt and inefficient prison administration. They attacked the absolute authority of the jail administrators and decried the housing of men and women together. The penal officials of the early nineteenth century could not, as yet, solve the problem of how to handle the mass of prisoners who came from the lowest parts of the social structure.

Many authors of the period believed that prison conditions were close to the living conditions of the lower classes on the outside and that this was the major reason for the rapid increase in the prison population. Prison conditions were too good! Or, at least, so believed penal theorists of the day. They felt that the lower classes committed crime in order to experience the comforts of prison life. Members of the working class came to believe this mythology: "Convicts are better off than we are; they throw more bread away than we can earn; they live a carefree life, feasting and drinking while we live in misery and cannot improve our lot." (quoted in Rusche and Kirchheimer, 1968:106). Many ruling-class theoreticians argued that progressive reform of prison life would not only reduce the deterrent effect of confinement, but would also provide an incentive for persons to commit crimes. The moderates argued that prisoners be accorded some improvements in their life, but *less than the rest of society*. Only a few individuals understood that the envy of the prisoner's lot reflected the degradation of the poor in the free society.

The consensus was that prisoners be given the barest minimum and that their level of subsistence be held below that of the poorest worker. Related to this idea of minimum subsidy was the growing notion that mere deprivation of liberty was no effective punishment for the lower classes. A prison report written in 1825 stressed that the necessary condition for the prisoner's reentry into society was *unconditional submission to authority*.[7] Prisoners, it was asserted, must learn to adjust to a regular, quiet, and industrious life. Inmates would be changed by exposure to *routines* that would lead to the development of proper habits. As far as possible, release ought to be based upon some guarantee of continued improvement on the outside. Penal administrators demanded obedience both to ensure smooth functioning of the prison and, perhaps more important, *to teach the convict to submit willingly to the fate of the lower classes on the outside*. Few believed that the wretched mass of prison inmates could be greatly elevated, but this did not prevent attempts at practical personal reform. For example, one prison gave inmates credits for additional bread if they refrained from consuming their portion immediately. The inmates were taught to conserve scarce resources, even in times of misery and want, in preparation of still worse times to come.

The principle that the living conditions of prisoners be kept below that of the lowest free classes meant regular readjustments of prison allotments of food. As the plight of the working class continued to decline in the nineteenth century, so too did the plight of prisoners. There are reports of starvation and sickness due to the consumption of spoiled food in prison. Virtually no medical service was available, and official reports noted that 60 to 80 percent of prison deaths were from tuberculosis. The mortality rate of prisoners was over three times that of a comparable age group in the general population.

Bad prison conditions, deliberate starvation of prisoners, and the steadily increasing convict population were accompanied by a change in the system of convict labor. Prisons and houses of correction were no longer profit-making entities. Many prison managers went bankrupt or abandoned their enterprise. Prison revenues were no longer adequate for the upkeep of prisoners or their jailers. Mechanizations in many industries made prisoner hand work unprofitable. The practice of hiring out the labor of convicts declined in popularity as the state assumed primary control of the prisons. Rather than viewing prison labor as essentially productive, legislators began to seek ways to reduce the expense of operating the penal system. One economic measure used by the state was to employ retired army men to administer the penal system; actual officers provided a cheap and useful source of prison officials. This practice, in turn, led to the introduction of military discipline and order in the prison.

[7] To the present day, this principle has remained one of the major elements of correctional theory.

Intensive use of machinery and the factory system of the industrial era created the problem of competition on the open market between prison-made goods and the products of free labor. In the mercantile age, with the widespread shortage of labor power, this competition posed no great problem, but now convict work was vehemently attacked by both workers and employers. During this period the problem of labor surplus was greater in Europe than in America, and we thus see changes in the European penal system that would not develop until later in American prisons.

As industrialization and mechanization made human labor less valuable, prison officials tended to leave inmates with no work to perform. This development caused a reexamination of the question of the purpose of imprisonment. Out of the debate over methods of penal treatment came the idea that work could be organized as *a form of punishment.* Reformers of the age argued that work for profit permitted inmates to associate freely with one another and thus launch criminal plans for the period after their release. Work as punishment would be guided by the principles of obedience and discipline and would lead to moral uplift.

Prison work evolved into a system of torture: penal officials invented occupations that were purely punitive and purposely fatiguing, and applied them for inhumanly long periods of time. "Prisoners carried huge stones from one place to another and then back again, they worked pumps from which the water flowed back to its source, or trod mills which did no useful work." (Rusche and Kirchheimer, 1968:112) Many prisons assigned convicts to treadmills (the "everlasting staircase") or grinding machines that ground sand and pebbles. The work of prisoners was no longer a source of cheap labor; rather, it was a means of debunking the notion that jails were places of refuge from bitter conditions on the outside.

Judges in this period did not appear to trouble themselves with issues such as fixed terms of incarceration or with exact principles of penal philosophy. Prisons as places of hunger, corporal punishment, and hard labor were designed to control the dangerous impulses of the poorer classes. Imprisonment meant more than the mere deprivation of liberty: it included pain and hardship.

Solitary Confinement

One of the most significant events in nineteenth-century penal practice was the institution of solitary confinement as a form of punishment. The use of solitary confinement in Europe provides yet another example of the relationship between punishment and social-structure change. As we shall see, the growth of solitary confinement and several resulting developments marked a shift in the major locale of penal reform to the United States.

Prison conditions in the United States were very similar to those in European prisons, as described in the preceding section. Fiscal considerations were important and the various American penal systems welcomed a plan to reduce the financial drain caused by prisons. One idea was strongly supported by the Quakers in Philadelphia, and it incorporated many of the ideas of the French cleric Mabillon. The central idea was solitary confinement: prisoners were isolated in single cells, which they never left until their prison term had elapsed or until they died or went mad.

The Quakers believed that religion was the basis of moral reformation, and they expected that solitary confinement would bring the offender-sinner back to God. Prisoners were locked up and not even allowed to work so that they could devote all their waking hours to contemplation. Prison officials permitted bible reading as well as visits with "pious persons" who would attempt to win the convict's soul back to God. Interaction among prisoners was restricted because it was believed that incorrigible criminals would corrupt others. Proponents of solitary confinement argued that the only true deprivation of liberty could be attained through a system of rigid inmate segregation. Self-examination, self-knowledge, and personal reform were the assumed results of the system, but some justified the practice because they believed that prison labor could not be made profitable.

Despite the zeal of its advocates, the "Pennsylvania System" was soon abandoned in nearly every jurisdiction in which it was adopted. Some observers have stressed the severe psychological problems experienced by inmates kept in solitary confinement; but the more important reason for the demise of the Pennsylvania System is that a great demand for workers existed in the northern states of America during the early nineteenth century—even greater than during the mercantile age in Europe. Slave importation was restricted by new legislation, land was available for exploitation, and the rapid industrial development created a labor need that could not be filled by the influx of immigrants. Work was available and wages compared favorably with those in Europe. Many Americans believed full employment to be a major reason for an allegedly low crime rate.

Upon release, convicts had little difficulty in finding work at favorable wages.

With such a prevailing economic picture, criminal justice administrators thought it ridiculous to keep prisoners in solitary confinement and thus waste their labor. In 1829 Pennsylvania prisons introduced work for all inmates, and this proved quite profitable. But work was restricted to what each prisoner could do in his own cell, and this limited the profit that could be extracted from prison labor. Penal reformers argued that machinery should be introduced into prisons to make labor competitive with outside manufacturing.

The "Auburn System" of New York State seemed the obvious solution to the dilemmas of penal practice of the day. The essence of the Auburn System was solitary confinement at night and collective labor in workshops during the day. These machinery vastly increased convict productivity, and, thus, nearly every American prison shifted to the Auburn System. The Quaker penal philosophy was given some recognition: prisoners were forced to work in complete silence and often wore black hoods to mask their identities so that convicts would not form criminal gangs once they were released. In contrast to the European situation, penal labor in America continued to produce profit and was never designed to be purely punitive.

Entrepreneurs often contracted for convict labor. First, a lease system that allowed capitalists to take complete control of prisoners during working hours was implemented, but this was gradually replaced by a "piece-price" system that left supervision in the hands of prison officials. The Civil War created a tremendous need for cheap clothing and footwear, and this demand caused a further increase in the use of prison labor. Special prisons were built for the purpose of housing long-term and short-term prisoners separately, for the labor of the former could be exploited more profitably. Reports show that the new prison system was self-supporting and often produced small profits.

The Auburn System introduced the practice of using privileges and rewards rather than discipline to encourage convict productivity. Good behavior by inmates could be measured by the amount of work performed. In 1817 New York State enacted a law that permitted all prisoners sentenced to more than five years in jail to earn a reduction of one quarter of their sentence by good behavior. This and similar laws constituted a powerful control mechanism for penal administrators because the possibility of commutation tended to reinforce the system of prison discipline and served as a substitute for the payment of money wages to convict workers.

Led by organizations of free laborers, opposition to convict labor grew in the latter decades of the nineteenth century. Wherever unions gained sufficient power to influence state politics, they curtailed prison industry: in some instances they succeeded in abolishing all convict labor, but the general result of their efforts was an end to the introduction of modern machinery into prisons and an end to the practice of giving prison goods to the state rather than selling them on the free market.

In Europe the surplus labor pool produced a different use of solitary confinement than in America. Prisons remained practical symbols of the cruel fate that might face an unruly working class. Reformers such as Elizabeth Fry, Stephen Grellet, and Mathilde Wrede continued to push for solitary confinement as a means of rehabilitating inmates, in lieu of a system of corporal punishment. They perceived solitary confinement as a powerful psychological tool toward the end of personal reformation. Prison officials, however, saw in solitary confinement a means of maintaining strict prison discipline. The older congregate system produced many prison riots in protest against harsh treatment, but solitary confinement made the prison easier to govern. Penal administrators argued for architectural changes in prisons so that inmates could be strictly segregated. In prisons that could not afford such modifications, the silence system was used. As time passed, the advocates of solitary confinement triumphed in many European nations. The solitary system made labor nearly impossible; but as we mentioned earlier, convict labor in Europe was not in demand, because of the general labor surplus. Rather, prison officials invented devices to make work punitive. The "crank" was a particular favorite in England. Sand would be poured into the crank to make it harder or easier to turn. Attached to the crank was an instrument that measured the number of turns performed by the convict. Critics such as Charles Dickens attacked the use of solitary confinement for inflicting unknown damage on the minds of inmates, but the system continued. Solitary confinement became especially significant as a means of dealing with the "unusual individuals" who were not really suited for rehabilitation. These were generally the inmates considered the most dangerous and the inmates who resisted prison discipline. Solitary confinement evolved into a tool for maintaining control within the prison, punishing rebels, and threatening the poorer classes on the outside. Although the system was dressed in the ideologies of moral reform and national penal practice, solitary confinement was developed in Europe for the primary reason of suppressing the dangerous classes in an age in which surplus population made convict labor unnecessary for the economic system.

The Adult Reformatory in the United States

Auburn Penitentiary in New York State, which became the model for adult corrections in the United States, was the training ground for the noted penologist Zebulon Brockway.[8] Young Brockway served in various positions in prisons in the Northeast. He assumed positions of leadership, first as governor of the City and County Almshouse at Albany, New York, and later as warden of the Monroe County Penitentiary in Rochester, New York. He was particularly concerned with reducing the costs of prison administration and eventually making prisons self-supporting: "[With the] productive employment of prisoners, the public expenditure for prisons should be limited to the cost of providing the plant; the matter of selecting and organizing the prison industries became at first and naturally the central purpose of management at the new county prison. (Brockway, 1912:64)" In his writings and activities, Brockway emphasized that penal measures would be fiscally responsible and that "curative" results could be obtained in institutions designed for "the dependent, defective, and dangerous classes" (*Ibid.*, p.73). He became a national figure, well known to penal reformers and administrators and recognized as the leading advocate of the reformatory movement in the United States. With the support of over 300 lawyers, physicians, clergymen, supreme court judges, and other prominent citizens, Brockway drafted legislation for the first Indeterminate Sentence Act (1877) in New York State. The new bill was passed almost unanimously. Brockway was then appointed the first superintendent of the Elmira reformatory and was thus given complete freedom to experiment with his views about penal treatment. Brockway was the uncontested leader of American corrections for the last quarter of the nineteenth century.

Brockway's views about the nature of criminals had a profound impact upon popular images about the causes of crime. The touch-

[8] The author is indebted to the unpublished research of Martin B. Miller, "To Keep Until Cured," for information about Brockway and the reformatory movement.

stone of his ideas was that criminals were inferior—the products of physical, mental, and moral imperfections: "They are not, generally, reasonable beings, in such sense that national considerations habitually control their conduct, either before or during their imprisonment." (Brockway, in Miller, 1973:13) Part of this alleged inferiority was attributed to inheritance and part to early family experiences. For Brockway, the purpose of the reformatory was to train "individuals out of adjustment with their environment" to observe the law and the valued properties of the community. He favored an indeterminate sentence, one that would end when the felon gave evidence that his future behavior would be more conforming. Brockway developed a simple classification scheme for his prisoners, dividing them into those "with arrested development"; those who were more dangerous and who faltered in times of stress; and those deficient in moral sense—these persons were excessively immoral. He claimed to have skill in diagnosing and classifying offenders, basing this claim upon his interviews with new inmates at Elmira.

Brockway's use of corporal punishment brought him under frequent attack by the press and certain citizen groups. In 1900 public sentiment against corporal punishment led to his removal from office at Elmira. Despite repeated attacks upon his methods, Brockway firmly believed in physical coercion. His inmates had to progress, and those "few" who were unresponsive were treated through "bodily sensitiveness . . . harmless parental discipline." The indeterminate sentence, according to Brockway, required more control and coercion than other systems. To him, there was no other way of dealing with the "incorrigible" or habitual offender.

Brockway was most proud of the economic organization of prison labor at Elmira: "By 1880 Elmira was grossing more than a quarter million dollars from the production of 485 prisoners. Net profit was $62,610.49: yet, Brockway still felt the need to expand." (Miller, 1973:17) The state legislature reviewed Brockway's request for additional operating capital but denied it. Over the next eight years, both labor and business lobbied against the economic competition, and in 1888 New York prohibited all productive labor in state prisons. Brockway cited the reformatory value of prison industry, although evidence suggests he was more concerned that the institution was self-sustaining.

Unable to profit from penal labor, Brockway experimented with the military regime as a means of maintaining inmate discipline. In 1890 he selected sixty inmates for an "officers' training school." A month later Brockway had organized a regiment of eight companies, who drilled and executed battalion movements to the sound of military band music. Inmates received merits and demerits for their skill (or lack of it) in military drills. "To the already military-looking prison uniforms were added insignia of rank and dummy rifles." (*Ibid.,* p.18) Visitors from the International Prison Congress were reported to be greatly impressed by the drill performance of the Elmira regiment. Brockway soon incorporated more of military style into the administration of the Elmira prison. Courts-martial replaced disciplinary hearings, and penalties included reductions in grade, six-month delays in release time, monetary fines, solitary confinement, and corporal punishment. Brockway's desire to continue prison industry was partially satisfied by the establishment of a state-used system of industries—prison production was utilized by other government agencies and institutions.

Another component of Elmira's penal program was the mark system. Brockway used *time* as a way of controlling difficult prisoners. Prisoners gained or lost time credits towards release, depending upon their conformity to institutional rules. Later, Brockway added monetary incentives, in the form of a wage-earning system, into prison regimes. The money-mark system translated into dollars and cents the system of merits and demerits for proper behavior inside the prison walls. Brockway wrote of his system as follows:

> Under its terms a man is forced to make his own living by industrious application to his assigned labor, by studious habits and proper regard for the rules enacted for his government, and along such a path journey to the confidence of the management and to the opportunity to be put to the test in the outside world, with oversight relaxed, the principle of reliance on self-exertion and self-control thus inculcated in him.

We see in Brockway's mark system an early forerunner of behavior modification techniques that have flourished in prison systems in the 1970s, though these techniques are supported by the prestigious science of behavioral psychology. Brockway relied more upon an intuitive sense that such a system of reward and punishment could be a potent coercive technique, especially when backed up by solitary confinement and physical punishment of those who would not conform under routine disciplinary measures.

Education was a crucial element of Brockway's program at Elmira. The end of the extensive inmate labor system lent added incentive to educational programs that kept inmates from the "evils of idleness." The program consisted of lectures and "student" debates on the subject of ethics. Convicts were to learn the moral values of the age and to develop the qualities of mind that would enable them to make correct moral judgments.

Brockway maintained an interest in the results of scientific experiments aimed at curing the most incorrigible inmates. Dr. Hamilton Wey was the most famous of the medical experimenters at Elmira who pursued means for the "moral betterment" of inmates. Dr. Wey's experiments involved exercise, massage, special baths, and military drills. Great claims were made for the miraculous improvement of selected inmates. Another prison experimenter, Dr. Elliot, attempted moral reform through dietary alterations. The results of such experiments were not astounding, but Brockway nonetheless believed that medical and physical treatments of prisoners could effect their moral and mental advancement.

Brockway and the New Penology

Brockway's practices at Elmira gained international recognition and aroused demands for penal reform in many European nations. It is important to note that few of his "innovations" were completely original; many elements of the Elmira program had been practiced in some form in the penal colonies during the last stages of the transportation system. Still, at Brockway's Elmira prison we see much of what remains contemporary penal practice. The indeterminate sentence, state-use industry, military routines, the mark system, the use of time as a disciplinary device, and experimentation on inmates—these are familiar elements of the modern state correctional facility. Moreover, Brockway's idea that penal practice should be individualized and oriented towards "prevention" continued to have much support among correctional administrators. What Brockway lacked, a seemingly objective basis for applying his penal treatments, was later provided by credentialed behavioral scientists and "helping professionals" who utilized the developing fields of psychiatry and social psychology to justify the various means handling of prison inmates. Intelligence tests, psychological measures, and casework methods provided the new techniques of selecting individuals for treatment by various penal methods.

Brockway's penal reforms spanned an era first characterized by labor shortage; but later the massive waves of European immigration and the industrial revolution in America made prison labor superfluous. Earlier objections to penal labor on grounds of unfair competition were replaced by an actual surplus in the labor pool. Without the need for the productive employment of convicts, America faced the dilemma of European nations that had experienced the industrial revolution years earlier.

The reformatory was one of several strategies employed by the privileged in the first decades of the twentieth century to control the dangerous classes. The increasing number of European immigrants presented a threat to the American white privilege structure, which imagined the prospects of racial extinction and the rise to political power of "inferior races" of people. The American privileged class debated plans to resist the alien invasion, and its spokesmen argued for measures designed to control the population of those they deemed "unfit." The perceived atmosphere of impending doom for the white race brought forth proposals to sterilize the mentally defective, the insane, and the criminal classes. Believing that inferiority was the defining aspect of criminals, social theorists postulated the core of American penal theory in the "Progressive era." According to famed sociologist E. A. Ross, "As to the mass of small-witted, weak-willed, impulse-ridden human 'screenings' that collect in prisons, our care should be to reform the reformable and to hold fast the incurable, the rest of their days" (Quoted in Miller, 1973:30).

At the turn of the twentieth century, both Americans and Europeans were immersed in debates over the most effective methods of controlling the dangerous classes. The once-powerful ideology of laissez-faire, which preached against too much state intervention, lost strength among members of the elite classes who were obsessed with fears of class struggle, race extinction, and the decline of the white, capitalist privilege structure. Calls for reforms and active planning for scientific social control pervaded the fields of education, welfare, mental health, and criminal justice. To find many of the ideologies and contradictions that plague our modern "welfare state" requires historical research into the developments of this period. It is significant that the young discipline of criminology experienced major growth at this very time. The new scientists of crime and crime control were called upon to construct theories and programs that would enable the dominant elite to cope with real and imagined threats to its hegemony. Perhaps the most important contribution of the new criminologists was to justify the ruling class's overlooking of the relationship between social injustice and the apparent threat to the social order. Treatment of the dangerous classes was shrouded within ideas of individual treatment, programs to induce social conformity by the downtrodden, and explanatuons of social evil that focused upon the personal troubles deriving from the milieu and thus helped mask the public issues of social structure, such as racism, economic exploitation, and other forms of social oppression.

Breaking the Chains of the Past

In this chapter we have presented a brief history of the development of penal practice in Europe and the United States. The narrative illustrates how the ruling classes of various epochs attempted to control those whom they believed presented the greatest threat to the existing privilege system. From the Middle Ages to the turn of the twentieth century, changes in penal policy and practice may be seen to be strongly related to changes in social structure. Such dislocations in social structure—whether due to changes in the labor market, alterations in basis for social status, or struggles for power among various groups—shape the way in which the powerful respond to the challenges of the powerless. Penal practice represents one of the various methods by which privilege is maintained and strengthened. We chose to focus upon systems of punishment because in this area the exercise of power and control is most directly observable. Alternatively, one might review the changes in legal codes or the transformations of social theory since the Middle Ages. Each of these areas of institutional change reveals different aspects of the dialectic between privilege and the quest for social justice. In time, the historical research of the New Criminology will flesh out the totality of the social-structure changes that have occurred in the past. But to reiterate an earlier point, the purpose of such historical inquiry is to provide insights that will aid change-oriented practice in the present.

There are several omissions in this historical narrative of penology and social structure. For example, we have not discussed the development of probation and parole systems, nor have we discussed developments in the control of juvenile delinquency. These are two crucial areas, which are currently being studied by a number of scholars. We ended our narrative at the turn of the twentieth century because social-structure changes in the past seven decades must be explored and analyzed more fully before we can comprehend the modern period completely. The economic and social transformations of the last seventy years are exceedingly complex, and this cautions us against "instant analysis." Still, the historical legacy of six centuries of penal practice weighs heavily upon the modern correctional system. The reader who is familiar with contemporary descriptive accounts of penal practice will recognize the themes and ideologies from the past that persist in the present. To break the chains of the past means to understand a legacy of penal ideology that has constrained creative thinking about humanistic methods of limiting the social costs of crime. If we are trapped by the thinking or eras long passed, the path to change is difficult if not impossible to find. Consider the extent to which ideas from the sixteenth, seventeenth, and later centuries continue to define the issues that are debated by modern penologists and criminal justice administrators.

If we can understand the relationship between punishment and social structure within the broader theoretical context of crime and privilege, perhaps we can escape from the mental prisons that prevent us from resolving the contradictions that plague our social institutions. At the least, we can escape the idealism and mystification that is the legacy of most standard histories of punishment and social control. And, thus, as we attempt to understand daily events and recent trends in criminal justice, we can more properly utilize our knowledge of the past to consider alternativies to the present approaches to the problem of crime. Viewed in terms of the interplay of power, privilege, and social-structure change, penal policy allows us to decode what is going on about us. It also reveals to us the primacy of the ideals of social justice in forming new approaches to the personal troubles generated by the public issues of an inequitable social structure. This is the promise of the sociological imagination as applied to the New Criminology.

FIVE

The Quest for a New Criminology

Once there was a way—or so it seemed—to get there from here.

Richard Quinney, 1974

Doing criminology—that is, studying crime and criminal justice, planning reforms, and helping persons caught up in the criminal justice system—seemed, not so long ago, a fairly straight forward task. However, developments in recent decades have blunted liberal optimism. As Quinney observed, "All we [once] had to do was to follow our procedures; all would be well. But then we began to understand." (Quinney, 1974: v)[1] As social scientists committed to the application of new knowledge to social relations, we were confronted with the nightmares of political murders, race riots, increasing political repression, and the moral dilemmas of a tragic war in Southeast Asia. In this period most of the powerful and most of the officials of the criminal justice system became symbols of the reactionary mode that appeared to settle upon the nation. In this period the liberation struggles of oppressed peoples, particularly

[1] The procedures were contained in the methodological wisdom of social-science research techniques. The assumptions, both theoretical and practical, were contained in the disciplines of law, sociology, psychology, political science, and social work. A generation of criminologists began the serious task of convincing political leaders, criminal justice officials, and the public that there were more rational and humanistic methods of reducing crime. Our optimism was tempered by the fact that we could only suggest our ideas to those more powerful, but we retained faith that progress, albeit slow, was inevitable. We were disgusted over the horrid conditions in prisons and the evidence of racial prejudice in the criminal justice system, but we believed these conditions would be gradually changed.

people of color, created the greatest tension in our consciences. Committed as we were to civil rights, racial equality, and social justice, how could we interpret the role of the criminal justice system in suppressing dissent, enforcing human misery, and preventing social change? The theories we had learned did not seem to apply; the history we had taken for granted was disputed and shown to be full of lies. Many of our scientific heroes of the past, upon rereading, turned out to be racists or, more generally, apologists for social injustice. In response to the widespread protests on campuses and throughout society, many of the contemporary giants of social science emerged as defenders of the status quo and vocally dismissed the claims of the oppressed for social justice. The crisis of disbelief widened and deepened as some of us felt compelled to understand "what was going on within ourselves and within our society."

The war in Vietnam was especially crucial in raising questions about the absolute moral validity of laws. The actions of political leaders strained credibility to the breaking point. Liberation efforts of black Americans and other third-world peoples presented a profound challenge to the "cherished" notions of equal opportunity, assimilation, and the benevolence of the liberal state. Organized struggles by women and other oppressed groups heightened our awareness of stereotypic thinking and dehumanizing social relationships. Particularly important for criminologists was the justification of political repression in the name of law and order. Prisons across the country erupted in riots and protests by inmates. In Attica, New York we witnessed the brutal massacre of inmates and guards by a penal administration believed by many to be quite progressive. As Richard Quinney observed, "Other sources became necessary."

This book does not represent a full-blown new theory of crime or social control. Any such claim would be pretentious as well as misleading. The New Criminology is in the process of becoming, and at this point we can only speculate as to future developments. At this stage the raising of questions is more appropriate than the facile giving of "answers." Above all, the New Criminology must avoid the complacent and doctrinaire quality of traditional research on crime. Remaining open to debate and dialogue among many persons is a difficult but necessary requirement for the New Criminology. It would be easy for us to slip into small camps of believers who clutch tightly to different ideological positions. In this sense the growth of our new approach to understanding crime requires us to participate in struggles for social justice. Moreover, we must never presume to speak for those who have not selected us to do so. Ideally, out of the dialogue and dialectic of ongoing struggles for social change will come the fresh insights, the clues for theory construction, and the priorities for research and practice.

The perspective which we have offered in these pages should be judged in terms of its utility in stimulating thought and discussion. In Chapter One, for example, we suggest an approach to *doing* criminology that departs from the conventional wisdom of social-science methods. Specifically, we interpreted the scholarly approach of C. Wright Mills in the belief that the infusion of the sociological imagination into the field of criminology might lead us to a more liberating form of social inquiry. Applying the sociological imagination requires, among other things, a sensitivity to the relationship between personal troubles and public issues; an increased awareness of historical research; the incorporation of moral objectives into the goals of research, achieved through the involvement of the scientist in change-oriented action, a redefinition of the relationship between the scholar and persons engaged in change-directed struggles; and the commitment to make one's research relevant to the quest for social justice.

Chapter Two, "Crime and Privilege," which includes rudimentary observations about the nature of crime, attempts to apply the principles of the sociological imagination to the study of crime. The main point of this chapter is that crime and crime control should be understood in terms of the public issues of social structure. Particularly, the New Criminology ought to examine ways in which the needs of the powerful and the maintenance of the privilege structure are reflected in the phenomenon of crime and the traditional approach to its study. We should look closely at the crimes of the powerful and of the role of the state as a partner to privilege. Our intention in this chapter was to discuss important concepts that may help explain the contradictions of crime and justice that confront us. For example, we tried to show the distinction between individual justice, or formal legal rationality, and social justice. This line of inquiry points to the necessity of studying the nature of criminal laws and law in general. For example, we need to understand why certain behaviors are strictly prohibited and how these "criminalized" behaviors are, in turn, related to the maintenance of privilege. Such areas of inquiry would benefit from both historical and cross-cultural research. We also briefly explored the cultural implications of crime. (Much work is needed in this area.) Finally, we discussed the relationship of power to criminal-justice decision making, suggesting that this be a fresh area of research.

Chapter Three was dedicated to the wisdom and courage of those who have struggled and continue to struggle on behalf of oppressed people. The content of that chapter is rich in information and insight. We must recognize the intellectual as well as political significance of Angela Davis, Eldridge Cleaver, the Panther 21, and George Jackson. If the New Criminology is to locate itself within the broader quest for social justice, its adherents must remain sensitive and responsive to the political and theoretical dimensions of the struggles of oppressed groups. We have little of value to offer these groups if we isolate ourselves from their ongoing struggles.

Chapter Four was not a brief history per se, but an effort to apply the ideas of crime and privilege to the development of penal philosophy and practice. Our task was greatly assisted by the monumental scholarship of Rusche and Kirchheimer in their classic *Punishment and Social Structure.* The New Criminology will continue this line of inquiry and hopefully extend historical understanding into other areas, such as the police, the judicial process, the formation of law, and the interface of criminal policy and social policy. Breaking the chains of outmoded ideology is important to the construction of a criminology committed to human liberation.

And where are we now? We must learn to tolerate the uncertainty that comes with each step away from imprisoning ideologies and practices. In criminology, one often hears the story of the inmate who has spent so much time behind bars that the decisions of free life are too painful. The New Criminology will likely be plagued with false steps and self-doubts, but the promise of the new approach that we have sketched will hopefully make up for the costs. The superstructure of privilege will not fall simply because some of us *will* it to be replaced. Moreover, the legacy of racism, sexism, and economic exploitation will complicate and frustrate many of our initial efforts. Building the New Criminology, decoding the processes of social control, and exposing the ideologies of privilege will be an extended and intellectually challenging effort that will engage many persons for several years to come.

The future of the New Criminology is both exciting and somewhat frightening. If we are no longer sure of *how* to reach the desired goal, it is important for us to admit this. But writers of the New Criminology such as Quinney and the British team of Taylor, Walton, and Young have presented some suggestions. Quinney, for example, argues that the path entails a struggle for a socialist society. He advocates extending Marxian analysis to the issues of our time in order to "remove our oppression and create a new existence" (Quinney, 1974:197). Quinney views the collapse of capitalism as inevitable but urges a collective effort to transform the society in which we live. Taylor, Walton, and Young briefly discuss practical issues in their *The New Criminology* and relate the new field to the support of the struggles of prisoners throughout the world. They assert that crime is behavior that always exists within the social framework and that this framework must change if crime is to be abolished.

> For us, as for Marx and for other new criminologists, *deviance* is normal—in the sense that men are now consciously involved (in the prisons that are contemporary society and in the real prisons) in asserting their human diversity. The task is not merely to "penetrate" these problems, not merely to question the stereotypes, or to act as "alternative phenomenological realities." The task is to create a society in which the facts of human diversity, whether personal, organic, or social, are not subject to the power to criminalize. (Taylor, Walton, and Young, 1973:282)

Their terminology and ideas are still new to us, and it is difficult at present to interpret the paths they envision or even to completely understand their ideal society.[2]

Unquestionably, the leaders of oppressed groups will enrich the New Criminology. Our common ground is the quest for social justice. It is crucial to understand that social justice does not mean that we all will become identical; rather, the basic principles of a social structure should be respect for the dignity of human life and the equal value of each individual. Practically, this means combating structures of institutional privilege and affirming the ideal of human liberation and self-determination.

[2] The New Criminologists of the Berkeley School of Criminology are in the process of developing approaches to the problems posed in theory and practice. One would expect that the continuing work of Anthony Platt, Herman and Julia Schwendinger, and Paul Takagi will result in a diversity of suggestions for theory development and participation in ongoing struggles. The last several years have produced the seeds of an engaging dialogue, which appears to remain open and may well lead to a maturing of the New Criminology perspective. The Berkeley group seems, at present, to place heavy emphasis upon involvement in community groups, efforts to organize prisoners' unions, and reform programs concerning the redistribution of power and resources throughout the society. In the future there will likely be more interaction among New Criminologists throughout the world as mediums of communication are developed and opportunities for discussion are enlarged.

Selected Bibliography

American Friends Service Committee. 1971. *Struggle for Justice.* New York: Hill and Wang.

Amir, Menachem. 1971. *Patterns in Forcible Rape.* Chicago: University of Chicago Press.

APTHEKER, BETTINA. 1971. "The Social Functions of Prisons in the United States." *If They Come in the Morning,* edited by Angela Davis. New York: New American Library, Signet.

BALBUS, ISAAC. 1973. *The Dialectics of Legal Repression.* New York: Russell Sage Foundation.

BALTZELL, E. DIGBY. 1964. *The Protestant Establishment.* New York: Random House.

BARAK, GREGG. 1974. "In Defense of the Poor: The Emergence of the Public Defender System in the United States, 1900–1920." D. Crim. diss., University of California, Berkeley.

BLAUNER, ROBERT. 1972. *Racial Oppression in America.* New York: Harper & Row.

BLUMBERG, ABRAHAM. 1974. *Current Perspectives on Criminal Behavior.* New York: Knopf.

BOOSTROM, RONALD. 1974. "The Personalization of Evil: The Emergence of American Criminology, 1865–1910." D. Crim. diss., University of California, Berkeley.

BOTTOMORE, THOMAS, ed. 1963. *Karl Marx: Early Writings.* New York: McGraw-Hill.

BROCKWAY, ZEBULON. 1912. *Fifty Years of Prison Service.* New York: Charities Publication Committee.

BROWN, CLAUDE. 1965. *Manchild in the Promised Land.* New York: New American Library, Signet.

BULLOCK, Henry. 1961. "Significance of the Racial Factor in the Length of

Prison Sentences." *Journal of Criminal Law, Criminology, and Police Science,* 52: 411–17.

BURKHART, KITSI. 1971. "Women in Prison." *Ramparts,* June: pp. 20–29.

CARTE, GENE. 1973. "August Vollmer and the Origins of Police Professionalism." D. Crim. diss., University of California, Berkeley.

CHAMBLIS, WILLIAM. 1973. "The Law of Vagrancy." *Warner Modular Publications Module,* 4: 1–10.

CLEAVER, ELDRIDGE. 1968. *Soul on Ice.* New York: McGraw-Hill.

CLOWARD, RICHARD, AND FRANCIS PIVEN. 1971. *Regulating the Poor.* New York: Pantheon.

COHEN, ALBERT. 1955. *Delinquent Boys.* Chicago: Free Press.

COMMITTEE FOR ECONOMIC DEVELOPMENT. 1972. *Reducing Crime and Assuring Justice.* New York: Committee for Economic Development.

COREY, LEWIS. 1930. *The House of Morgan.* New York: Grosset and Dunlap.

CURRIE, ELLIOTT. 1973. "Managing the Minds of Men: The Reformatory Movement, 1865–1920." Ph.D. diss., University of California, Berkeley.

DAVIS, ANGELA. 1971. *If They Come in the Morning.* New York: New American Library, Signet.

DENFELD, DUANE. 1974. *Streetwise Criminology.* Cambridge, Mass.: Schenkman.

DIRKS, RAYMOND, AND LEONARD GROSS. 1974. *The Great Wall Street Scandal.* New York: McGraw-Hill.

DIXON, MARLENE. 1972. "Academic Roles and Functions." *The Insurgent Sociologist,* 2: 8–17 (Spring).

DOMHOFF, E. WILLIAM. 1967. *Who Rules America.* Englewood Cliffs, N.J.: Prentice-Hall.

DOMHOFF, E. WILLIAM, AND HOYT BALLARD, eds. 1968. *C. Wright Mills and the Power Elite.* Boston: Beacon Press.

DUBOFSKY, MELVYN. 1969. *We Shall Be All.* Chicago: Quadrangle.

ERICKSON, KAI. 1966. *The Wayward Puritans.* New York: John Wiley.

FANON, FRANZ. 1968. *The Wretched of the Earth.* New York: Grove Press.

FREIRE, PAULO. 1970. *Pedagogy of the Oppressed.* New York: Herder and Herder.

FULLER, JOHN G. 1962. *The Gentlemen Conspirators.* New York: Grove Press.

GERTH, HANS, AND C. WRIGHT MILLS, eds. 1967. *From Max Weber.* New York: Oxford University Press.

GOLD, MARTIN. 1966. "Undetected Delinquent Behavior." *Journal of Research in Crime and Delinquency,* 13: 27–46.

GOLDMAN, PETER AND DON HOLT. 1971. "How Justice Works: The People vs. Donald Payne." *Newsweek,* March 8: 20–37.

GOULD, LEROY. 1969. "Who Defines Delinquency: A Comparison of Self-Reported and Officially-Reported Indices of Delinquency for Three Racial Groups." *Social Problems,* 16: 325–35.

GOULDEN, JOSEPH. 1970. "The Cops Hit the Jackpot." *The Nation,* 520–33.

GOULDNER, ALVIN. 1968. "The Sociologist as Partisan: Sociology and the Welfare State." *The American Sociologist,* May: 103–16.

GRIFFIN, SUSAN. 1971. "Rape: The All-American Crime." *Ramparts*, September: 26–35.

GUSFIELD, JOSEPH. 1968. *Symbolic Crusade: Status Politics and the American Temperance Movement.* Urbana, Ill.: University of Illinois Press.

HALBERSTAM, DAVID. 1972. *The Best and the Brightest.* Greenwich, Conn.: Fawcett.

HAYDEN, TOM. 1970. *Trial.* New York: Holt, Rinehart and Winston.

VON HENTIG, HANS. 1937. *Punishment: Its Origins, Purpose and Psychology.* London: William Hodge and Company.

HIRCHI, TRAVIS, AND HANNAN SELVIN. 1967. *Delinquency Research: An Appraisal of Analytic Methods.* New York: Free Press.

HOROWITZ, IRVING LOUIS, ed. 1967. *Power, Politics and People.* New York: Oxford University Press.

JACKSON, GEORGE. 1972. *Blood in My Eye.* New York: Bantam.

———. 1970. *Soledad Brothers.* New York: Bantam.

JANOWITZ, MORRIS. 1968. *The Social Control of Escalated Riots.* Chicago: University of Chicago Press.

JORDAN, WINTHROP. 1974. *The White Man's Burden.* New York: Oxford University Press.

KENNEDY, MARK. 1970. "Beyond Incrimination." *Catalyst*, 6: 1–37.

KNOOHUIZEN, RALPH, RICHARD FAHEY, AND DEBORAH PALMER. 1972. *The Police and Their Use of Fatal Force in Chicago.* Chicago: Chicago Law Enforcement Study Group.

KOLKO, GABRIEL. 1969. *The Roots of American Foreign Policy.* Boston: Beacon Press.

———. 1970. "The Unchanging Pattern of Inequality." In *Crisis in American Institutions*, edited by Jerome Skolnick and Elliott Currie. Boston: Little, Brown.

KRISBERG, BARRY. 1972. "Review of Laud Humphries' Tearoom Trade." *Issues in Criminology*, 7: 126–27.

———. 1974. "The Sociological Imagination Revisited." *Canadian Journal of Criminology and Corrections*, 16: 145–61.

LEFCOURT, ROBERT. 1971. *Law Against the People.* New York: Random House, Vintage.

LENIN, V. I. 1968. *State and Revolution.* New York: International Publishers.

LIAZOS, ALEXANDER. 1972. "The Poverty of the Sociology of Deviance: Nuts, Sluts and Perverts." *Social Problems*, 20: 103–20 (Summer).

LOGAN, CHARLES H. 1972. "Evaluation Research in Crime and Delinquency: A Reappraisal." *Journal of Criminal Law, Criminology and Police Science*, 63: 378–87.

LUKAS, GEORG. 1971. *History and Class Consciousness.* Cambridge, Mass.: M.I.T. Press.

MATZA, DAVID. 1969. *Becoming Deviant.* Englewood Cliffs, N.J.: Prentice-Hall.

MELVILLE, SAM. 1971. *Letters from Attica.* New York: Morrow.

MEMMI, Albert. 1967. *The Colonizer and the Colonized.* Boston: Beacon Press.

MESSINGER, SHELDON, et al. 1962. "Life As Theatre: Some Notes on the Dramaturgic Approach to Social Reality." *Sociometry,* 25: 98–110.

MILIBRAND, RALPH. 1969. *The State in Capitalist Society.* New York: Basic Books.

MILLER, MARTIN B. 1973. "To Keep Until Cured." Criminology paper, University of California, Berkeley.

MILLS, C. WRIGHT. 1959a. *The Power Elite.* New York: Oxford University Press.

———. 1959b. *The Sociological Imagination.* New York: Oxford University Press.

———. 1956. *White Collar.* New York: Oxford University Press.

MITFORD, JESSICA. 1973. *Kind and Unusual Punishment.* New York: Knopf.

MORRIS, ALBERT. 1941. "Criminals' Views on Crime Causation." *The Annals,* 217: 138–44.

NEWTON, HUEY. 1973. *Revolutionary Suicide.* New York: Ballantine.

O'CONNOR, JAMES. 1973. *The Fiscal Crisis of the State.* New York: St. Martin's.

PALLAS, JOHN, AND BOB BARBER. 1972. "From Riot to Revolution." *Issues in Criminology,* 7: 1–19.

PETERSON, DAVID, AND MARCELLO TRUZZI. 1972. *Criminal Life: Views from Inside.* Englewood Cliffs, N.J.: Prentice-Hall.

PILIAVIN, IRVING, AND SCOTT BRIAR. 1964. "Police Encounters with Juveniles." *American Journal of Sociology,* 70: 206–14.

PLATT, ANTHONY. 1969. *The Child Savers.* Chicago: University of Chicago Press.

———. 1974. "Prospects for a Radical Criminology in the United States." *Crime and Social Justice,* 1: 2–10.

———. 1973. "Towards a New Criminology." Paper presented at the 1973 Meeting of the Pacific Sociological Association.

President's Commission on Law Enforcement and the Administration of Justice. 1967. *Task Force Report: The Police.* Washington, D.C.: Government Printing Office.

QUINNEY, RICHARD. 1974. *Critique of Legal Order.* Boston: Little, Brown.

———. 1970. *The Social Reality of Crime.* Boston: Little, Brown.

RAINWATER, LEE, ed. 1974. *Inequality and Justice.* Chicago: Aldine.

Report of the National Commission on Civil Disorders. 1968. New York: Bantam.

RUSCHE, GEORG, AND OTTO KURCHHEIMER. 1968. *Punishment and Social Structure.* New York: Russell and Russell.

RYAN, WILLIAM. 1971. *Blaming the Victim.* New York: Random House, Vintage.

SCHWITZGEBEL, RALPH. 1971. *Development and Legal Regulation of Coercive Behavior Modification Techniques with Offenders.* Washington, D.C.: National Institute of Mental Health Service Publication No. 2067.

SEALE, BOBBY. 1968. *Seize the Time.* New York: Random House, Vintage.

SELLIN, THORSTEN. 1944. *Pioneering in Penology.* Philadelphia: University of Pennsylvania Press.

SKOLNICK, JEROME. 1966. *Justice Without Trial.* New York: John Wiley.

SMITH, RICHARD. 1961. "The Incredible Electrical Conspiracy." *Fortune,* April: 132–80 and May: 161–224.

SNODGRASS, JON. 1972. "The American Criminological Tradition: Portraits of the Men and Ideology in a Discipline." Ph.D. diss., University of Pennsylvania.

TAFT, DONALD. 1942. *Criminology.* New York: Macmillan.

TAKAGI, PAUL. 1974. "A Garrison State in a Democratic Society." *Crime and Social Justice,* 1: 27–33.

TAYLOR, IAN, PAUL WALTON, and JOCK YOUNG. 1973. *The New Criminology.* New York: Harper & Row.

THOMAS, PIRI. 1967. *Down These Mean Streets.* New York: New American Library, Signet.

THUROW, LESTER C. 1969. *Poverty and Discrimination.* Washington, D.C.: Brookings Institution.

TONG, BEN. 1971. "The Ghetto of the Mind." *Amerasia Journal,* 1: 1–31.

TSE-TUNG, MAO. 1967. *Selected Works of Mao Tse-Tung.* Peking: Foreign Language Press.

TYLER, GUS, ed. 1962. *Organized Crime in America.* Ann Arbor, Mich.: University of Michigan Press.

WALKER, MARGARET. 1969. *Jubilee.* New York: Bantam.

WALLERSTEIN, JAMES, AND CLEMENT WYLE. 1947. "Our Law-Abiding Law-Breakers." *Probation,* April: 107–12.

WILDEMAN, JOHN. 1971. "The Crime Fighters." Ph.D. diss., New York University.

WILLHELM, SIDNEY. 1970. *Who Needs the Negro.* New York: Doubleday, Anchor.

WILLIAMS, ERIC. 1966. *Capitalism and Slavery.* New York: Capricorn Press.

WILLIAMS, GWYN. 1960. "Gramsci's Concept of Egomania." *Journal of the History of Ideas,* 21: 586–599.

WILLIAMS, JAY, AND MARTIN GOLD. 1972. "From Delinquent Behavior to Official Delinquency." *Social Problems,* 20: 209–29.

WOLFE, ALAN. 1973. *The Seamy Side of Democracy.* New York: McKay.

WOLFGANG, MARVIN, AND BERNARD COHEN. 1970. *Race and Crime.* New York: American Jewish Committee, Institute of Human Relations Press.

WOLFGANG, MARVIN, AND MARC RIEDEL. 1973. "Race, Judicial Discretion, and the Death Penalty." *The Annals,* 407: 119–33.

WOLFGANG, MARVIN, ROBERT FIGLIO, AND THORSTEN SELLIN. 1972. *Delinquency in a Birth Cohort.* Chicago: University of Chicago Press.

X, MALCOLM. 1964. *Autobiography of Malcolm X.* New York: Grove Press.

ZINN, HOWARD. 1970. *The Politics of History.* Boston: Beacon Press.

Index

Q

R

S

T

V

W

X

Y